We are all climbing different paths through the mou[ntain...]
And we have all experienced much hardship and stri[fe...]
There are many paths through the mountain of life
And some climbs can be felt like the point of a knife.
Some paths are short and others are long
Who can say which path is right or wrong?
The beauty of truth is that each path has its own song
And if you listen closely you will find where you belong.
So climb your own path true and strong
But respect all other truths for your way for them could be wrong.

—DAN INOSANTO

Jeet Kune Do

The Art and Philosophy of Bruce Lee

by Dan Inosanto
with Alan Sutton

Library of Congress Catalog Card No.: 76-26986
ISBN: 0-938676-00-8

KNOW NOW PUBLISHING COMPANY
3932 So. Hill St., Los Angeles, CA 90037

Dedication

I dedicate this book first and foremost to the memory
of Bruce Lee, my Si-Fu, in the art of Jeet Kune Do.

Then I dedicate it to:

Linda Lee, Bruce's wife, to Brandon and Shannon Lee,
Bruce's children, to Mrs. Grace Lee, Bruce's mother,
with the hopes that they will realize the impact,
influence and love that Bruce Lee had upon the disciples
of Jeet Kune Do,

To my mother and father, Mary and Sebastian Inosanto,
who gave me life and taught me to appreciate it,

To my wife Sue, and my children Diana Lee and Lance
Inosanto, with the hope that they will treasure the material
as I treasure them,

To the memory of James Lee, my Si-Hing (older brother)
in the art of Jeet Kune Do,

To Taky Kimura, my Si-Hing in Jeet Kune Do,

To Richard Bustillo, my training partner and friend for
influencing me in the continuation of the lineage of
Jeet Kune Do,

And to my Jeet Kune Do students and my Filipino Kali
students, for without them I could never grow.

—DAN INOSANTO

Contents

Introduction

"Like an iceberg—one-tenth above water, nine-tenths hidden below—the art of Kung-Fu stretches far beyond the more visible combat techniques into the very fibers of the Chinese culture. Born from the twin influences of Taoism and Zen, the way of life that is Kung-Fu stands as a practical application of these philosophies. Fighting forms that might never be used during a lifetime take on added meaning as vehicles to a higher goal—striving not for injury or death to another, but an increase in the capacity for life. Years of hard training soon transcend mere combat in the search for harmony with the universe. . . ."

—INSIDE KUNG-FU magazine

"JKD can become intelligible only in the process of self-discovery."

—BRUCE LEE

The classics (writings and traditions) provide modern man with a link to the wisdom of the ancients, but in themselves are just the product of an earlier genius. To be bound by tradition is the way of the mindless, the enslaved. To be inspired by tradition to achieve further heights is the way of genius. And herein lies the "secret" of Bruce Lee's unique contribution to the martial arts—Jeet Kune Do.

A devastating amalgam of speed, power and deception—Jeet Kune Do stands alone as today's only nonclassical form of Chinese Kung-Fu. What sets JKD apart from all other forms is the absence of stereotyped techniques; it is alive, fluid, continually adapting. Sometimes it resembles Western boxing. At other times it looks like Thai kickboxing; or fencing, Judo, Filipino Escrima, even wrestling ("Absorb what is useful; reject what is useless; add what is specifically your own," Lee used to say). Still, it is rooted in the timeless precepts of Taoism and Zen which form the basis of Chinese boxing. *Jeet* means to stop, to intercept. *Kune* means fist or style. And *Do* means the way or the ultimate reality.

The ultimate achievement in Jeet Kune Do is not the wholesale destruction of one's foes but rather the annihilation of things that stand in the way of peace, justice, humanity. The art thus becomes the embodiment of life and not of death. Or as Lee once told a writer for *Esquire*: "A punch or a kick is not to knock the hell out of the guy in front, but to knock hell out of your ego, your fear, or your hang-ups."

The fact is, Jeet Kune Do for him was not an end in itself, nor was it merely a by-product. It was a means of self-discovery. JKD is a prescription for personal growth, or to put it another way, it is an investigation of freedom—freedom to act naturally and effectively, not only in combat, but in life. "Art lives where absolute freedom is," wrote Lee. He realized that like any other art, the martial arts demand self-knowledge and expressed the idea that character, like the body, could be shaped to make it more symmetrical and beautiful.

Lee devoted a lifetime to the development of an all-encompassing martial arts philosophy. Early on in his teaching career he explained to his students: "Mere technical knowledge of Gung-Fu [Cantonese spelling] is not enough to make a man really its master; he ought to have delved deeply into the inner spirit of it." His many years of training and discipline had convinced him that the real purpose for studying a martial art is for self-improvement. Searching for the ultimate reality on combat, he uncovered certain truths about the meaning of life and refused to canonize them into set rules or formulas because, as he used to caution his disciples, "My truth will not be your truth."

And Lee was not content only to instruct: he wanted to inspire his followers to think along with him. He wanted them to develop what he termed a "discerning mind." He understood that a precept is wholly true "only insofar as it is experienced and lived in the present." So unless his students joined in the "problem solving," which was how he sometimes described JKD, they could not understand it. They had to dig, participate actively; thus Lee's concepts are kept alive, his ideas fresh. "A good teacher," he wrote, "functions as a pointer of truth, but not as a giver of truth."

Lee also rejected the notion that learning is a process of accumulation. It is in reality the opposite, he said, using the analogy of a sculptor who instead of adding clay to his subject, keeps chiseling away until the essence is revealed. In other words, Jeet Kune Do involves a daily decrease rather than increase. Truth can only be realized once you have discarded all the untruths or "inessentials," as he called them.

Lee had no desire to found a new style. "On the contrary," he informed the readers of *Black Belt* magazine in August 1971, "I hope to free my comrades from bondage to styles, patterns and doctrines." He was no savior. He wanted nobody to take his word as gospel; he knew that a martial artist is first and foremost a man: "Man, the living creature, the creating individual, is always more important than any established style or system." He despised the word style because it presupposed separateness and division, when life is really organic and whole.

Every style is self-limited, whereas Truth is universal. Instead of any revolutionary system, Lee wanted the truth—the whole truth as well as all styles, soft as well as hard, internal as well as external, the physical as well as the spiritual, life as well as death and in the end, Man at one with the never-ending Tao.

The purpose of this book is to clear up the numerous misconceptions, misrepresentations, misstatements of fact and inaccuracies surrounding Bruce Lee and his art of Jeet Kune Do. Since Bruce's death, the Jeet Kune Do organization has purposely maintained a low profile, wanting no part of the burgeoning Bruce Lee market that now includes T-shirts, patches, emblems, posters, medallions, comic books, uniforms, several low-budget celluloid ripoffs, uninformed magazines, books, etc.—all of which have nothing whatsoever to do with the man or his art. In truth, there are only three places in the entire world that offer instruction according to authentic Jeet Kune Do principles:

The first is Seattle, Washington, where Bruce's longtime

friend and associate, Taky Kimura, teaches at a private club in the basement of his grocery store.

The second is Charlotte, North Carolina, where Larry Hartsell, who has trained in JKD since 1967, teaches a few select students at a friend's Kung-Fu school.

And the third is the Filipino Kali Academy in Torrance, California, where Dan Inosanto and his partner Richard Bustillo, through much financial sacrifice and personal denial, have established perhaps the finest, best-equipped martial arts center in the world.

It is not the intention of this book to depict Bruce Lee's life story in words and pictures. It does, however, attempt to show his influence on a whole generation of people.

We hope that by tracing the origins and development—and illustrating some of the basic principles—of Jeet Kune Do, this book will present fresh material not found in any of the existent literature. Ideally, it will bridge the gap left by Bruce's unfinished masterpiece, *The Tao of Jeet Kune Do,* and other books which focus primarily on his public life and movie career.

But it is *impossible to capture the truth of Jeet Kune Do in a book; its implications reach to the very crux of life.* We have merely tried to shed some light on the process Bruce Lee was so reluctant to name because he felt it would be misconstrued as just another form of Karate or Kung-Fu. The important thing to remember is that for him, Jeet Kune Do meant freedom—the kind that comes from having no illusions about yourself or your potentials.

THE PUBLISHERS

Conversation with the Author

"Bruce Lee was by no means perfect—he had his short-comings—but in my opinion, he was truly a highly evolved individual," says Dan Inosanto. "The thing that impressed me most about Bruce was not his physical skill; it was his knowledge—of life as well as martial arts."

For years Inosanto was a close personal friend and sparring partner of the consummate martial artist who became the first Oriental superstar by clobbering all comers in films like *Fists of Fury, Chinese Connection, Enter the Dragon* and *Return of the Dragon*, only to die unexpectedly in 1973 before his 33rd birthday. One of three men originally authorized to teach Lee's art of Jeet Kune Do, Dan modestly plays down his own ability. "At 40, I think I hold my own," says the five-foot, five-inch Filipino-American welterweight. "But that's only a small portion of it. I was just in the right place at the right time, and I was willing to sacrifice at any length to study under Bruce." He adds: "I don't even feel I'm the best in JKD." Apparently, however, Lee didn't see it that way, because upon leaving for Hong Kong in the early Seventies to make a name for himself on the Mandarin circuit, he left Inosanto with a "flexible" game plan for the perpetuation of Jeet Kune Do. "I had a lesson plan that was not to be rigid. Like he set up certain principles on speed, balance, weight distribution, etc., that are true regardless of the method or style, but he wanted me to incorporate my own innovations," Inosanto recalls.

Like Lee, Inosanto is a martial artist by choice, securing his livelihood through other means. Currently he teaches physical education and driver's training in the Palos Verdes School District not far from his home in the Los Angeles suburb of Harbor City. He lives with his wife Sue, their two children—Diana, 10, and Lance, 6—and a German shepherd named JKD. And four nights a week he conducts classes at the Filipino Kali Academy, which he started up in March 1974 with fellow Bruce Lee student, Richard Bustillo. He says his primary concern is to promote the indigenous arts of

the Philippines—Escrima, Panantukan, Kali, Arnis, Sikaran—while using the facility for the further development of Jeet Kune Do. "Here we're able to kill two birds with one stone," Dan explains. "We can advance the Filipino arts—which have been pretty much ignored up until now—and have the gym be the center for JKD functions, too.

"I like both arts," he continues. "I consider them two halves of one whole. They complement each other; and to us, the Kali has opened our eyes in JKD and vice versa." Beginning students are taught a modified form of Wing Chun Kung-Fu, supplemented with boxing fundamentals, Escrima hand techniques, and Panantukan. And as they progress they are introduced to Kali and Jeet Kune Do. Says Inosanto: "We feel that these are the two highest stages of our art."

Before he ever met Bruce Lee, Dan was already an accomplished martial artist in his own right; having studied among other things: Judo, Jiu-jitsu, the Filipino arts, of course, and several styles of Karate. Born in Stockton, California, he was first exposed to Okinawan Te (meaning "empty hand") at the age of 10 by an uncle who was also an Escrimador, as it turns out. Then he took up Judo during summers home from Whitworth College in Spokane, Washington (where he was a standout in track despite his size) and was later bombarded by a potpourri of styles as a paratrooper stationed at Fort Campbell, Kentucky. In Dan's opinion this was a definite plus, establishing a pattern of cross-training that has since become his personal trademark.

Returning to civilian life in 1961, Inosanto enrolled in a Kenpo Karate class under the direction of renowned West Coast instructor Ed Parker. After three more years of intensive study, he finally received his *shodan* (black belt) at 28 and became one of Parker's assistants. Universally regarded as the Father of American Karate, Parker has nothing but praise for his former employee. "Danny was a very good student," he says. "He was also very observant and absorbed as much as he could from everyone he came into contact with. I gave him little bits and pieces, then let him figure the rest out for himself. Being an educated kid, everything soaked in."

Even as late as the time when he began studying Kenpo, Dan still regarded martial arts as nothing more than an enjoyable pastime—offering body conditioning and self-defense, that's all. Shortly afterwards, however, once his cultural and martial identities started to merge, he realized that there was more to it than "just slam, bang, punch and kick," he says. Discovering that his ancestors—as well as the Chinese, Japanese, Koreans, Okinawans, et al.—possessed a rich and colorful heritage all their own, provided the foundation that Bruce Lee would later expand upon.

"I began to see the truth in martial arts—that it represents a microcosm of life—when I was with Ed," notes Dan. "He asked me one day, 'Have you ever seen the art of Escrima?' And I said, 'You mean stick fighting.' He said, 'No. There's more.' That's what started me thinking."

Sparked by Parker's lecture, Inosanto sought vehemently for persons versed in the Filipino arts, simultaneously keeping up his Kenpo studies. In his hometown of Stockton, he uncovered five Escrimamen: Max Sarmiento, Regino Elustrismo, Gilbert Tenio, Angel Cabales, and Jon Lacoste. Constantly on the lookout for additional instruction, he was able to train with a number of other experts who were little known outside the Filipino community, including Pasqual Ovalles, Pedro Apilado, Leo Giron, Dentoy Revillar, Braulio Pedroy and Subing Subing. In fact, his travels have taken him as far as Hawaii, where today many of the leading practitioners make their home.

"In my opinion," offers Inosanto, "the leading exponent of Kali is in Hawaii; his name is Floro Villabrille. I studied with his foremost student, Ben Largusa." With a hint of pride in his voice, he elaborates: "Now by their definition, Kali is the highest art of the Philippines. It's an empty hands art, but most people mistake it for a stick art. And also, in many ways it even surpasses Jeet Kune Do in the 'trapping' stage.

"This art was in the Philippines before the coming of the Chinese during the T'ang Dynasty," he continues adding a historical footnote. "Magellan was killed by it. He was killed, you see, with a rattan stick—not a sword like the history books say." As for any type of ranking system, Dan explains: "The authority to teach is given by handing down a favorite weapon or pet movement; there are no credentials."

Inosanto is also indebted to Parker for another reason, for it was at the latter's International Karate Championships in 1964 that he—and the rest of the world for that matter—was introduced to Bruce Lee. Parker had flown Lee down from Seattle, Washington, to put on a demonstration of the as then unknown art of Kung-Fu, at the tournament which was held in Long Beach, California. Dan was competing in the black belt division, and after the matches were concluded he had the opportunity to exchange techniques with Bruce back at his hotel room. He remembers feeling less than pleased at the results of their brief sparring session:

"I couldn't sleep that night; I was really bothered because it [Lee's fighting style] was something that I'd never seen before. It was like having learned an occupation for many years and then having someone say, 'We no longer have any use for you.' In my case, I'd studied all these different arts—I won't say that it was worthless—but what he did was counter everything without really trying."

The tournament took place in July, and for the remainder of the year Inosanto saw quite a bit of Lee. "I toured with him after the first Internationals because Taky [Kimura] had to go back to Seattle. We swung up through San Francisco, and gave exhibitions. I learned from him while he stayed at the Statler Hilton in L.A. where I dummied and took falls for him for four days during demonstrations at the Sing Lee Theater. In the process, he taught me what at that time was his system [a devastatingly modified form of Wing Chun; Jeet Kune Do had not yet been conceived]."

Lee returned to the Los Angeles area again in 1965, and Twentieth Century-Fox put him on retainer for the following year in anticipation of the upcoming *Green Hornet* series. As a result, he had lots of free time on his hands and, as Inosanto recalls: "That was when I got the brunt of my training. I must have pestered the heck out of him, coming to his house week in and week out—and even on Sundays. He worked with me for a whole year and introduced me to three Chinese guys. We were the only ones training under Bruce at that time. Then he found a little place on College Street [in Los Angeles' Old Chinatown] and said, 'I think I'll start a school.' "

With acting lessons, filming and promotional tours taking up more and more of his time, Lee was forced to relegate most of the teaching chores over to Inosanto. The only problem was that Dan still continued to teach for Parker—and he admits he began to feel the strain. "For two years I taught simultaneously for both Ed Parker and Bruce Lee," he winces. "But I was married and I had no family life. I was teaching three nights a week for Ed Parker and four nights for Bruce Lee—that was no life for my family. So I began to taper off with Ed simply because I had more responsibilities."

In the beginning, though, Dan wasn't entirely certain that he'd made the right choice. "The first few months I was with Bruce Lee were very frustrating," he concedes. "He seemed really cocky, and at first I wasn't sure if I would like him as an instructor. In the beginning I wanted to stay with Ed and just get all the information I could from Bruce. But then things began to blossom into a friendship rather than a student-teacher relationship. I became very close, very attached to Bruce. I just dug being around him, that's all." Indeed, for Dan named his first child, a girl, Diana Lee, after his now famous buddy.

Diana Lee Inosanto with JKD.

In stark contrast to his famous sifu (instructor), Dan Inosanto can truly be called humble and self-effacing. Content to remain in the shadows and not bask in Bruce's fame, his idea of a good time is to remain after class into the wee hours of the morning jawing with students or friends. Essentially opposites, if Bruce was yang, then Dan must be yin.

"I probably look upon Bruce now as more of a philosopher than a martial artist," he reveals. "Although I think the two are deeply entwined. When I was training with him I thought he was too philosophical; but as I look back on it, I just wasn't prepared for what he had to say. After his death I began to understand more, because I knew there was no one I could rely on for the answers. Since '73 I've discovered things that have made my Escrima 100 percent better—that's my JKD. Having studied with Bruce, I begin to see how the principles of Jeet Kune Do hold true no matter what. Bruce used to say, 'Life is combat.' And that's why everything we learned could be applied elsewhere."

Wing Chun-the Nucleus

In setting up his art Bruce Lee seems to have acknowledged the fact that there is nothing so permanent as change. Down through the years some things stayed the same, but there was continual modification. For example, when I first met Bruce back in 1964, he had by then considerably altered his original style, Wing Chun.

Upon returning to the States from Hong Kong at the age of 18 (Lee was born in San Francisco), he began almost immediately to adjust the angles, stances and footwork of Wing Chun because it was too "rigid," as he put it. The end product of all his experimentation, which he called Jun Fan (a variation of his Chinese name), was the art that was taught at the schools he opened in Seattle and Oakland in the early Sixties. And though he considered this new art to be more fluid and direct than its predecessor, Bruce always expressed a very high opinion of Wing Chun. Indeed, even after he had taken it a step further to create Jeet Kune Do, he would still say: ". . . I would like to stress the fact that though my present style is more totally alive and efficient, I owe my achievement to my previous training in the Wing Chun style, a great style."

Wing Chun (meaning "beautiful springtime") was reportedly founded by a woman, Yim Wing Chun, some 400 years ago. The style was based on the techniques of Shaolin nun Ng Mui of the southern temple in Fukien province.

But Yim Wing Chun felt that Ng Mui's style was too complex and placed too much reliance on power techniques and strong horse stances. She was looking for, instead, the simplest, least complicated, most efficient means of defending herself; and not finding it among the existing styles, she created her own.

Yim Wing Chun taught the art to her husband—an actor by profession who was also versed in the martial arts—and it was passed down through the centuries to Leong Bok Sul, Wong Wah Bo, Leong Yee Tai, Leong Jon, Chan Wah Soon, Yip Man (Lee's instructor), Leong Sheong and Wong Soon Sum.

Despite its roots deep within the legendary Shaolin Temples of Old China, Wing Chun comes to the twentieth century as one of the most modern styles of the ancient art of Kung-Fu.

Based on the theory that the shortest distance between two points is a straight line, Wing Chun lacks the elongated, flowing motions that are a part of most other forms of Kung-Fu. The centerline, an imaginary line that runs down the center of the body, forms the basis of Wing Chun movements—the axis around which the blocks and strikes revolve. Wing Chun practitioners are taught when in combat to have their centerline directly opposite the opponent's chin.

The immovable elbow theory, the four corners and *lin sil die dar* (simultaneous block and attack), contribute to the overall economy of movement which is characteristic of Wing Chun. The first of these concepts—which holds that the hand and forearm can move in any direction, but the elbow must remain in position about three inches in front of the body—defines the boundary lines for proper utilization of Wing Chun techniques.

The boundaries of the four corners are identical to those of the immovable elbow: the eyebrows at the top, the groin area at the bottom and the region just past the shoulders on either side. Also, the body is divided into four areas, or gates as they are called. And within each gate there is a forward area and a rear area.

Lin sil die dar, though quite simple in theory, is harder to implement in practice. As the natural tendency is to either retreat or try to block an attack, this concept can only be mastered after much training and discipline.

The simplicity of Wing Chun is reflected in the total number of forms (*kuens*) in the style—three! In one way or another, all Wing Chun techniques are contained within the *sil lum tao* ("little idea"), the *chum kil* ("searching for the bridge") or the *bil jee* ("shooting fingers").

Wing Chun training starts with *sil lum tao,* the basic foundation of all that will follow, and progressed through *chum kil* and *bil jee,* in that order. Along the way, the student is also taught the *chi sao* ("sticky hands") exercise. This exercise, based on the dynamic balance of opposing forces (*yin* and *yang*), heightens the student's sensitivity in his hands and arms to

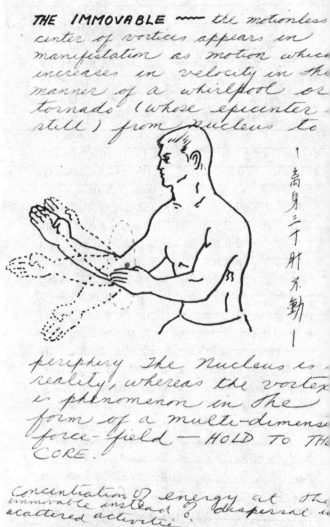

THE IMMOVABLE ～～ the motionless center of vortices appears in manifestation as motion which increases in velocity in the manner of a whirlpool or tornado (whose epicenter still) from nucleus to periphery. The nucleus is reality, whereas the vortex is phenomenon in the form of a multi-dimensional force-field — HOLD TO THE CORE.

Concentration of energy at the immovable instead of dispersal in scattered activities.

illustrations by Bruce Lee

20

The Ready Position (By-Jong 擺桩)
& The Three Gates 三門

upper Gate
上 門

Middle Gate
中 門

Lower Gate
下 門

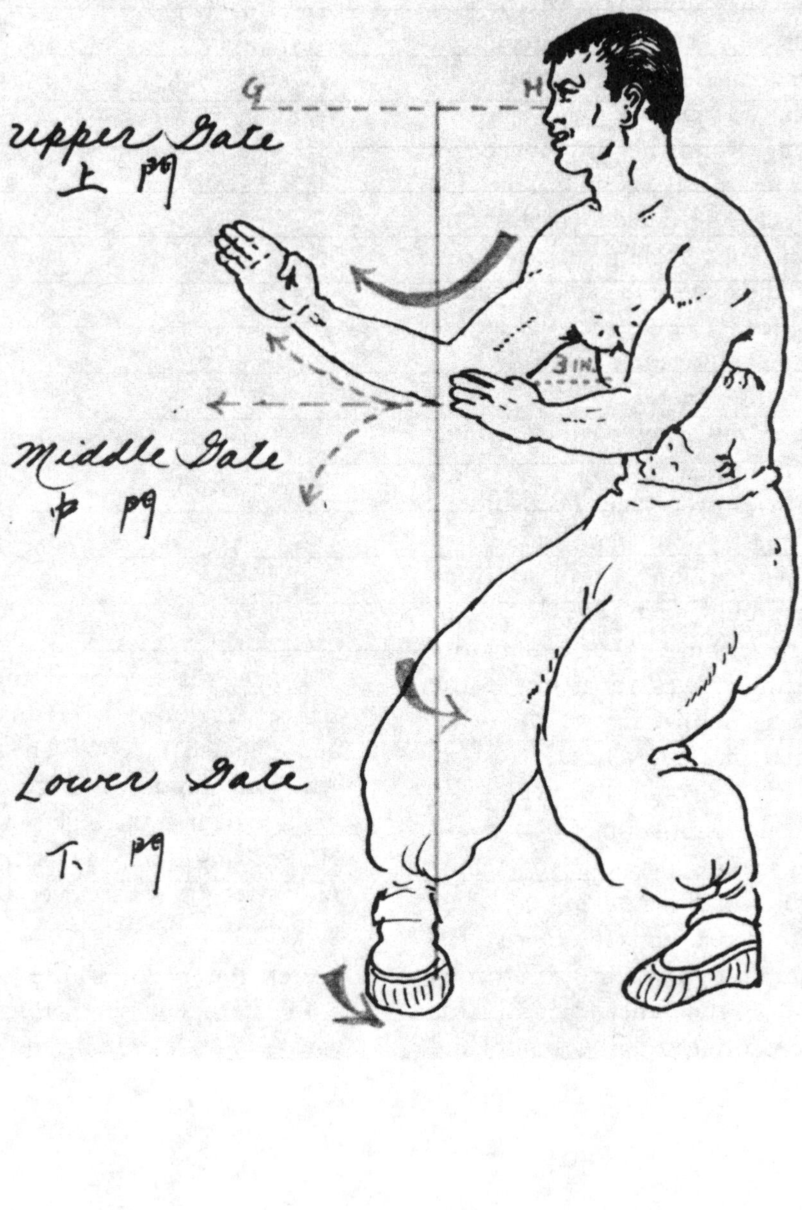

the point where he can detect the intentions of his opponent by feel.

Finally, after the three forms and *chi sao* have been mastered, the student applies what he has learned in the 108 movements of the *mook jong* (wooden dummy). A training method unique in all the martial arts, the 108 movements simulate every conceivable situation and stand as the pinnacle of Wing Chun training—all previous knowledge contained and applied therein.

Although Bruce's father had introduced him to the graceful flowing movements of Tai-chi when he was just a youngster growing up in Hong Kong, he did not begin training in earnest until he was about 13. As the story goes, he decided to take up Wing Chun out of a feeling of insecurity that arose once he had established a reputation as a gang leader and street fighter. "I kept wondering," he once confided to many of his close friends, "what would happen to me if my gang was not around when I met a rival gang."

So in the Fifties Bruce became a student of the famed master Yip Man, then patriarch of the Wing Chun school in Hong Kong—and he would go to any length to further his instruction. One of his favorite ploys, for example, was to arrive at the training hall long before any of the other students. And then as they began to show up for class, they would be greeted by Bruce who would assure himself of a private lesson by shaking his head and telling them, "The old man's not in. No class today." He also had friends in other styles, which gave him an opportunity to broaden his horizons as the energetic Chinese youths practiced tirelessly after school and

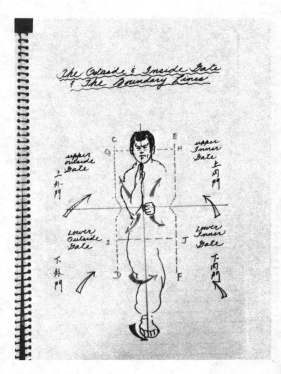

even during recess.

During his senior year in high school, Bruce developed a fascination for boxing and decided to enter an amateur contest. An uncommonly fierce competitor, his being crowned the high-school champion of Hong Kong is only surprising in light of the fact that he had never before put on a glove!

Yet the real purpose of the countless hours he spent sharpening his techniques with Yip Man's senior students and friends

Low block — facing or
half facing.
(Coming straight)
from immovable
2½ in.

Blocking — upper
outside gate
(from immovable)
2½ in.

3 in.
away from
center of
chest.

in other styles, as well as the experience he got in the unfamiliar confines of the ring, was purely structural: according to Bruce, the ideal proving grounds for combat remained the ever-dangerous backstreets and alleyways of Hong Kong.

Taking into account the myriad styles of Kung-Fu that were—and still are—taught openly in Hong Kong, why did Bruce select Wing Chun? From all indications I have gathered over the years, there were three things he liked especially about Wing Chun: (1) its economical structure; (2) its directness; and (3) its emphasis on energy or sensitivity training (*chi sao*).

In any event, I think it is safe to say that Wing Chun does in fact form the nucleus of Jeet Kune Do. For only with a basic foundation that is already stripped down practically to the essentials could he have made such rapid and amazing strides in the development of his own art, as we shall see in the following chapters.

Gung-Fu is training and discipline toward the ultimate reality in
self-defense, the ultimate reality is simplicity.
A true Gung-Fu never opposes force or gives way completely.
Be pliable as a spring. Be the complement not the opposition to
the opponent's strength. Make his technique your technique.
You should respond to any circumstances without prearrangement,
your action should be like the immediacy of a shadow adapting to
a moving object against the sun.
Your task is simply to complete the other half of the "oneness"
spontaneously. There is nothing to "try" to do, in the final stage
of Gung-Fu, opponents, self, techniques are all forgotten. Everything
simply "flows."
The true art of Gung-Fu is not to accumulate but to eliminate.
Respond like an echo. Adapt like a shadow. Strike like an arrow.
In Gung-Fu, it's not how much you have learned, but how much
you have absorbed. It is not how much knowledge you can
accumulate in Gung-Fu, but what you can apply in Gung-Fu.
One technique well mastered is more reliable than a thousand
half learned.

—BRUCE LEE 1964

Jun Fan - Liberation

For a time while he was a student at the University of Washington (circa 1962), Bruce seriously contemplated a nationwide chain of Kung-Fu schools. Several years later, when his spiraling Kato fame would have certainly ensured the success of such a venture, he discarded the idea saying that was not the way to bring out the art. And then as his movie career started to break, he realized that here was the proper medium for enlightening the public as to the true meaning behind the martial disciplines.

In the intervening years, though, Bruce did establish three *kwoon* in Seattle, Oakland, and Los Angeles respectively. Yet all were "non-commercial" to the extent there were no signs anywhere on the outside to identify them.

As I pointed out in the preceding section, when Bruce first came to America from Hong Kong he didn't waste any time in adjusting his system to fit the new environment. Indeed, he was astutely aware of the fact that the compact movements and close range tactics of Wing Chun, which were ideal for the overcrowded conditions in the Far East, were ill-suited to the sprawling metropolitan areas of San Francisco and Seattle—his first two stops.

To further illustrate the profound impact environment can have on one's method of fighting, I would only mention that there exists a style of Filipino swordfighting which teaches its practitioners to respond to an encounter by immediately dropping to the ground in a seated posture. Ridiculous, you say? Sure, if the assault takes place on solid footing, such as a parking lot or a deserted street corner. But there is an unusually heavy rainfall in the region where this style comes from, which leaves the ground so muddy and slippery that after the first stroke the practitioner would invariably slip down anyway.

So as he began to see that Wing Chun placed too much emphasis on close range or in-fighting (hand techniques) at the expense of long range (kicking techniques) fighting, Bruce incorporated some of the more refined kicks of the

Taky Kimura credits his success over much adversity in life and in international business to Bruce Lee's philosophy that "Life is Combat" and you must deal with it accordingly.

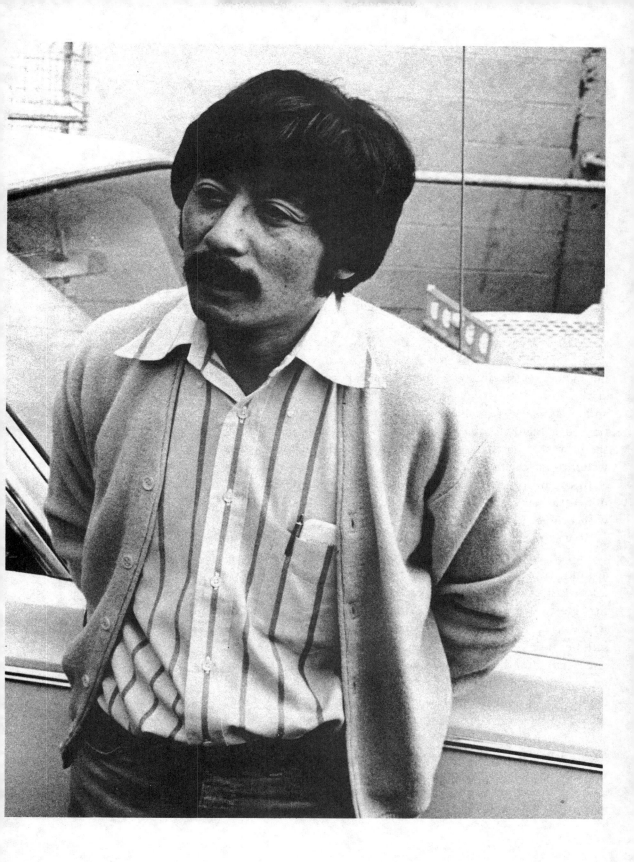

Northern Chinese styles. And it is this hybrid form of Wing Chun that today we refer to as Jun Fan.

Originally, though, the term Jun Fan was used to designate the school—not art—of Bruce Lee. You see, Jun Fan Gung-Fu Institute was the name Bruce gave to the non-commercial establishments in Seattle, Oakland, and Los Angeles; and later on the meaning again shifted somewhat to mean "the place where Jeet Kune Do trains." Then once Jeet Kune Do was firmly established as an entity in itself, Jun Fan was looked upon as the art that Bruce taught in Seattle and Oakland—which was more Wing Chun oriented with additional kicking techniques. Jeet Kune Do, then, is really a liberated form of Jun Fan; it encompasses much more. But Jun Fan is still part of the total art. You can't separate the two.

His wife Linda recalls that Bruce started impromptu teaching in the Seattle area even before he was officially enrolled at the University of Washington. Blessed with superior talent and a dynamic personality, it's not surprising that he attracted a highly visible—if small—group of devotees. Among them was a Japanese-American named Taky Kimura, then well into his thirties (Bruce was not yet twenty).

In the process of researching this book, I visited with Taky in Seattle where he recalled how he first became acquainted with Bruce and his art:

"I was taking Judo around 1959. And I got hurt two or three times so it was pretty frustrating. In fact, I was running around with my arm in a sling when one of the fellows that knew Bruce dropped by the supermarket where I was working. He told me he'd met this young man from Hong Kong who was 'phenomenal'. Of course, I took it with a grain of salt because by that time I'd seen a little bit of everything and I couldn't believe there was anything more to be seen. During that time these guys were working out in backyards and in public parks. So I went to one of the athletic fields down by the university, and that's where I first met him. I was so impressed when he unleashed his power and speed that I asked if I could join the group and for about a year we met for several hours on Sunday. After class we would go to a Chinese restaurant and listen to Bruce philosophize over a cup of tea."

Taky Kimura shows us the living quarters of Bruce Lee while he stayed in Seattle, Washington. He lived in the attic of Ruby Chow's restaurant. The photo's for his CHINESE GUNG FU book were shot in the parking lot next to the restaurant.

By this time, too, Bruce was becoming increasingly disenchanted with his setup at Ruby Chow's. A Seattle restaurant owner and prominent figure in local politics, she had consented to let him stay in one of the rooms above her restaurant in exchange for his services as a busboy and waiter. But, as Taky recalls: "Ruby Chow could be a very domineering person and, in fact, Bruce could be too. So I think there was a little personality clash, and he recognized that it was time to get out of there. But Bruce was also a very proud young man and felt that he had to make it on his own rather than become a burden on his father by having him send money. And since he was endowed with all this knowledge of martial arts, the guys in the group he was training gathered together and decided to open up a school and try to get some money for him."

Taky also remembers trying to impress upon the young instructor the fact that, in spite of his age, he was Bruce's most dedicated and determined student—and how it eventually paid off. "I was working twice as hard as the other guys," he explains, "because I was much older than them. One day I was looking out of the corner of my eye to see if this made any impression on Bruce. Of course, he knew exactly what I was doing and I heard him say to one of the other guys: 'He'll never make it.' Naturally this drove me to try that much harder. And even though I was very clumsy, I think he saw that I was very dedicated and sincere in what I was trying to do.

"Then he started to work with me and kind of took me aside and showed me a lot of extra things. The next thing I knew he was grooming me to be his assistant. As time wore on, I did become his assistant instructor, and more or less conducted all his classes.

"The first school was down in Chinatown, simply because, I suppose, we were more familiar with that area than anywhere else and it was a smaller group at that time. Shortly thereafter, we recognized the limitations of the Chinatown location and since he was going to the university, we felt there would be more potential out that way."

So the Jun Fan Gung-Fu Institute was relocated along University Way, prompting Bruce and his assistant to step up the

To be humble to superiors, is duty; To equals is courtesy; To inferiors is nobleness; And to all, Safety!

The doer alone learns.

Diseases enter by the mouth, misfortune issues from it.

Simplicity is the end of art, and the beginning of nature.

—BRUCE LEE

This was the first training establishment Bruce opened in Chinatown, Seattle, Washington.

This is my favorite picture of Bruce. He often gave prints of this to his senior students.

One of Bruce's many original drawings.

Taky Kimura of Seattle, Washington, shows Richard Bustillo and me
Bruce Lee's third Jun Fan Gung Fu Institute school near the campus
at the University of Washington. Today it houses the "Truth Center."

This underground passage
hid the second, fourth and
last Jun Fan Gung Fu Institute
in Seattle Chinatown.

demonstrations they had been giving on campus and at various fraternity houses in hopes of drumming up additional business. Initially they were quite successful and were able to maintain what Taky terms "plush" headquarters in a ground floor studio that was part of a brand new apartment complex. The enrollment fee was twenty-two dollars per month or seventeen for juniors.

During one of Bruce's early demonstrations, a Japanese Karate black belt took exception to his outspoken opinions and ideas and issued a challenge. Bruce tried to explain that it was not his intention to downgrade any particular system but rather to clarify his own methods. But the Karate expert persisted in demanding a bout, telling the sizable crowd that had gathered around that Bruce didn't "know anything. Don't listen to this guy." So Bruce was forced to accept the challenge, and the two departed for a nearby handball court. The challenger wanted first to establish certain ground rules, such as no punching to the head or groin, and going against his usual practice, Bruce accommodated him to an acceptable degree. Still, the outcome of the brief (11 seconds) match was never in doubt. The Karate man opened with a strong kick

Today Taky Kimura still teaches a select group in his private club located beneath his supermarket.

which Bruce effortlessly avoided before punching his opponent from one end of the court to the other. When it was all over, the challenger lay in a pool of blood. And, as Taky explains, Bruce was quite magnanimous about the whole affair. "The Karate guy was out of school for a whole week after the fight and when he came back, he told all his friends that he'd been in a car accident. Rather than embarrass him any further, Bruce just let it go at that."

Taky says the Institute continued until around 1963, or about the time of Bruce's marriage to pretty blonde coed Linda Emery. By then there was a considerable turnover of students, and Bruce decided that the best thing to do would be to return to Chinatown with a small core of dedicated followers. "It was a good move at that point," explains Taky, "because shortly after that he left Seattle and, hell, I wouldn't have been able to keep up that big place by myself.

"Bruce and I were discussing it one day after he had moved to California, and we decided not to promote the school as such. He said: 'Why don't you just close it down? After all, what's life about than to have some close friends around who you can trust?' So I continued on that basis. Today, we operate only as a very exclusive private club."

The Jun Fan training roster in Seattle.

Taky Kimura demonstrates the use of one of his pieces of training apparatus in the basement of his Seattle Gym for Richard Bustillo.

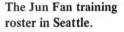

JUN FAN GUNG FU INSTITUTE

BRUCE LEE SCHOOL OF SELF DEFENCE

GENERAL RULES

- Arrive promptly for class.

- Pay dues on time.

- Maintain personal cleanliness.

- Keep the school clean. DO NOT KICK THE WALLS.

- Stand at the position of attention while receiving orders from the INSTRUCTOR or from an ASSISTANT INSTRUCTOR. Respond immediately to such instructions.

- Be cautious while practicing. Do not overwork yourself while exercising, and do not experiment with new techniques without supervision.

- Do not smoke in the school. If you smoke at all, it will slow your progress in gung fu.

- Learn the Chinese names for general commands and for all the techniques you know.

- Exercise discretion when explaining to others about this school. Do not engender ill feelings or rivalry with students from other schools.

- The INSTRUCTOR is here to teach you and to answer your questions. However, do not bother him with trivia. If you have any doubts, ask an assistant instructor first.

All students will read and obey these rules. Intentional disobedience will result in expulsion.

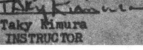

Taky Kimura
INSTRUCTOR

Less than a year after the close of the Seattle *kwoon*, the newlyweds had moved into James Lee's house in Oakland. A widely respected martial artist in his own right, James was probably the first classically trained Kung-Fu man in America to recognize and appreciate Bruce's extraordinary ability. In fact, it was at James' suggestion that Bruce had been asked to appear only months before at Ed Parker's International Karate Championships, which proved to be the major turning point in his career.

Bruce Lee, Ed Parker and James Lee in the early 1960's discussing techniques.

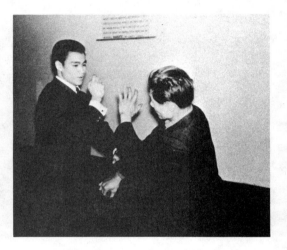

Bruce and James Lee in a spontaneous workout with their business suits on.

Actually it was fate that originally brought James and Bruce together near the end of 1962. As it turns out, the pair were introduced through James' relatives who had been taking dancing lessons from Bruce on and off since his arrival from Hong Kong in the late Fifties. (Bruce's stay in San Francisco was a short one. He supported himself by teaching the cha cha before accepting Ruby Chow's offer of steady employment.) Allen Joe, who grew up with James and was a good friend of Bruce's, explains:

"James' brother Robert was taking dancing lessons and during intermission, Bruce gave a demonstration of Wing

Chun. So he went home and told James that Bruce had put on a pretty good show. At that time James paid no attention; we were taking our classical style and felt like hotshots in Kung-Fu. Then James said to me, 'Since you're going to Seattle'—this was for the World's Fair in 1962—'why don't you check this guy out and see how good he is?'"

"When I got to Seattle," Allen Joe continues, "I looked him up at Ruby Chow's restaurant. I waited until after eleven that night, then finally he showed up. I was sitting there having a Scotch, and in walked Bruce all dressed up real sharp. No smile. He must have been wondering what in the heck I was doing there. So right away I mentioned Bob's name and he relaxed. We started talking Kung-Fu and went out back where he told me to go through my classical motions. Then he said real calmly, 'That's no good. Now try it again.' And I went flying all over the place; I was really impressed. After that he went through his routine on the wooden dummy (*mook jong*), which he had set up in the parking lot behind the restaurant. And I was even more impressed watching him work on the dummy. He was so smooth that everything I had learned seemed stiff and clumsy in comparison.

"After I returned home, Bruce wrote me a letter, and about two weeks later, James wrote him and he came down for a visit. Ever since then he and James became good friends. Bruce started teaching James his version of Wing Chun, and James said: 'Allen, this guy is good. He's *unreal!*' That was the beginning. Then James and Bruce continued training together and eventually opened a gym."

The gym Allen Joe refers to became the second Jun Fan Institute. (It was located on Broadway and has long since been torn down to be replaced by a Pontiac dealership.) Like Bruce, James had little patience for stoics in the martial arts community who still clung to the outmoded belief that the secrets of Kung-Fu should not be revealed to non-Chinese. Both men agreed to accept students from all races in their *kwoon,* which caused resentment and antagonism among some of the die-hard traditionalists.

Bruce felt that by creating his own method he could avoid the fierce interschool rivalries which had been a way of life in

These training devices were designed and constructed by James Lee for the art of Jeet Kune Do. The one on the left is a punching device that snaps back when you hit it. The two in the middle are for training the finger jab (Biu Jee) and the half knuckle jab (Choap Chue). The device on the right is a stationary head used for punching and striking.

The finger jab device is mounted on the wall and set for a man at 5'10". It can be adjusted to a height of 6'10".

The opening portion of the finger jab device when it is hit by the half fist. The bottom half, under the chin, simulates a man's throat.

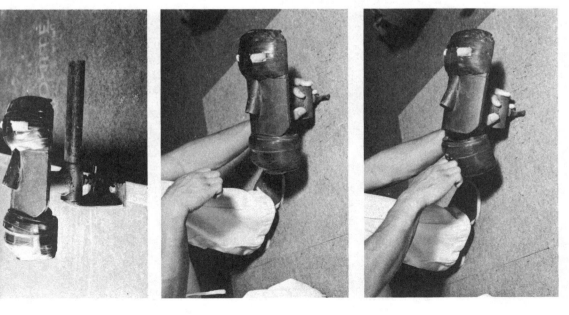

Portrait of James Lee as a young man. He was a highly skilled martial artist, writer, welder and inventor. His innovations, inventions and talents have been immeasurable in the art of Jeet Kune Do.

The finger jab apparatus in use. The picture on the right illustrates a right finger jab to the eye.

Hong Kong. This was only wishful thinking, however. And one of the first experts to attempt to put Bruce in his place was a Kung-Fu master from across the Bay in San Francisco's Chinatown.

Wong Jak Man had recently arrived from Hong Kong and was looking to establish a name for himself. Accompanied by some of his followers, Wong turned up at the Institute one day with a written challenge informing Bruce that if he lost the ensuing fight, he was to either close down the school or stop teaching Caucasians.

Apparently the challenge was an ultimatum from the San Francisco martial arts community. "I'm representing these people here," Wong admitted pointing to his followers. Bruce's reply was simply: "OK, then"—which had an unsettling effect on the intruders who figured Bruce would likely back down from a serious challenge by a skilled boxer like Wong.

Bruce then became incensed when Wong suggested that they simply spar lightly for a few minutes. "I'm not standing for any of that," he fumed. "You've come here with an ultimatum and a challenge, hoping to scare me off. You've made the challenge, so I'm making the rules. So far as I'm concerned, it's no-holds-barred. It's all out."

One of the few eyewitnesses to the scene that followed was Linda Lee, then eight months pregnant. She reports that "within minutes" Wong's men were trying to stop the fight, as he was ignominiously running from Bruce. The farce ended as Bruce dragged his challenger to the ground and pounded him into submission.

Until the clash with Wong Jak Man, Bruce had for the most part been content to improve and expand his original Wing Chun style. All that changed, though, when he began to dissect the fight and realized that his rather lackluster performance (the fight should have lasted only seconds) was due in large measure to his thick-headed adherence to a style which his opponent's Law Horn Kuen techniques were impervious to. In addition, as Bruce confessed to the author some years later, he was unusually winded near the end which proved to him that he was in less than perfect shape. So partly because he recognized once and for all the limitations

Alan Joe reflects on the many pleasant experiences he shared with Bruce. He attributes much of his philosophy and outlook on life to these experiences.

This was the former garage and house of James Lee in Oakland. It was in this garage that James held his classes in Wing Chun, Gung Fu and Jeet Kune Do. I enjoyed regular visits with Bruce to Jame's house for almost a year and one-half. Bruce and I always looked forward to flying to Oakland to train and to be with James.

George Lee, Bruce, Alan Joe and James Lee on the "Green Hornet" set. It was George Lee who made the famous "Classical Mess" tombstone for Bruce.

Bruce enjoyed the relaxed atmosphere in Oakland.

The Lee family were regular customers at Alan Joe's market.

of Wing Chun, and partly out of a growing appreciation of the need for proper conditioning—Bruce began to intensify his search for the ultimate reality in combat. And if there was one thing he had learned from his many years of experience and training, it was that the myriad forms of martial arts all relied on styles that were essentially incomplete. Or as Linda Lee succinctly observes in her fascinating and informative book titled *Bruce Lee: The Man Only I Knew*:

"Each had its own forms, movements and so on and each practitioner went into battle believing that he had all the answers and for that reason he [Bruce] refused to call Jeet Kune Do a 'style' which he felt would be to limit it. As it was, therefore, it possessed neither rules, a set number of forms or movements or a set number of techniques with which to oppose other techniques."

As for conditioning—it was in this area that Bruce perhaps picked up a few tricks from James. A champion weightlifter and gymnast in his youth, James had trained with such outstanding physical culturists as Jack La Lanne, Steve (Hercules) Reeves, Clancy Ross, and Japanese Olympic titlist Tommy Kono. Also, he was a welder by trade and responsible for turning out many of the mechanized training devices that Bruce used to develop his amazing power and force.

"Credit James," says Allen Joe, "with getting Bruce interested in body building. I don't think he started serious weight training until after he met James. Even though his system was based on elusiveness and speed, he still believed that you had to have some strength. In fact, he used to overtrain: He used to do reverse curls all day long with a pair of dumbbells to develop his forearms. Then later he bought a set of weights and began training regularly." Again, as with the art itself, Bruce put the accent on simplicity and efficiency. "He would pay careful attention to the location of the different apparatus—where to put the squat bar, the bench press, etc.," explains Allen Joe.

With the aid of Taky Kimura and James Lee, Bruce had given countless exhibitions and demonstrations throughout the western United States prior to the summer of 1964. Still the art remained little known outside of America's Chinatowns, and Bruce debuted it to the world that year at the

Many people thought of James Lee as a physical person only. FIGHTING ARTS OF THE ORIENT and MODERN KUNG-FU were just two of the books he wrote which displayed his ability to express himself intellectually.

A book that Bruce Lee wrote in 1963 showing various techniques from Chinese systems of Gung Fu. He considered this book to be not the best in quality. However, he believed the section on the basic theories of the Yin and Yang were informative.

This picture hangs on the wall at the Filipino Kali Academy. It reads, "To Dan, my Si Dai in Jeet Kune Do - word master denotes a slave, style manifests itself in narrow horizons and bondage. It is only when master and style are transcended that true freedom of expression begins. Your Si Hing, James Yim Lee, 11/24/72."

The original Mon Fat Jong (thousand way dummy) that James Lee created for kicking and various hand techniques for Bruce. It is an ingenious device with car springs and shock absorbers that cause an unusual life-like effect when you kick it. The arms and legs are not attached in this photo, but they are always there when you work with it, just like a real person always has an arm or a leg for you to deal with. I later inherited this dummy from James Lee.

To James.

Circumstances! Hell, I make circumstances

Take it easy (on the brandy that is ....)

Bruce Lee

Bruce gave this portrait of himself to James Lee.

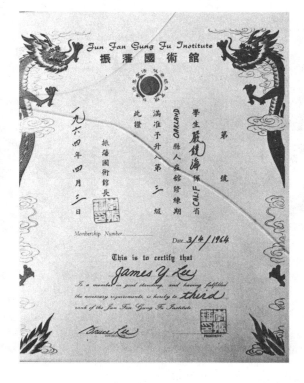

This is James Lee's diploma, making him third rank in the Jun Fan Gung Fu Institute.

The former location of the Oakland Jun Fan Gung Fu Institute,
where the battle with Wong Jak Man took place, is now a car dealership.

inaugural edition of the International Karate Championships —dazzling the thousands of spectators with his superb skill. Fortunately, Ed Parker was on the sidelines getting it all down on film.

"I had it in color and sound, and I kept it hoping I could use it someday," Parker now recalls. "Then a year or so later, I was teaching Jay Sebring. Jay and I were good friends and we were talking about the need for a guy to play Kato, because Jay's friend was Bill Dozier, the producer of *Batman*. He [Dozier] had purchased the rights to the *Green Hornet*, and he needed a Kato. The producers wanted someone who knew the art. So I made arrangements to take the film to Bill Dozier, and Bill looked at it and said, 'That's the guy I want' —Bruce."

Next Bruce was contacted by Dozier, who had him fly to Los Angeles for a screen test and as a result he was signed to an option for the coming year. The Institute wasn't showing much of a profit—for the reason Bruce was a perfectionist who would only admit serious students and then teach them on a one-to-one basis—so it was moved to James' garage in late 1965.

And shortly afterwards, looking ahead to a promising career in television, Bruce decided to move his family (his son Brandon had just been born) to Hollywood.

Jeet Kune Do – Freedom

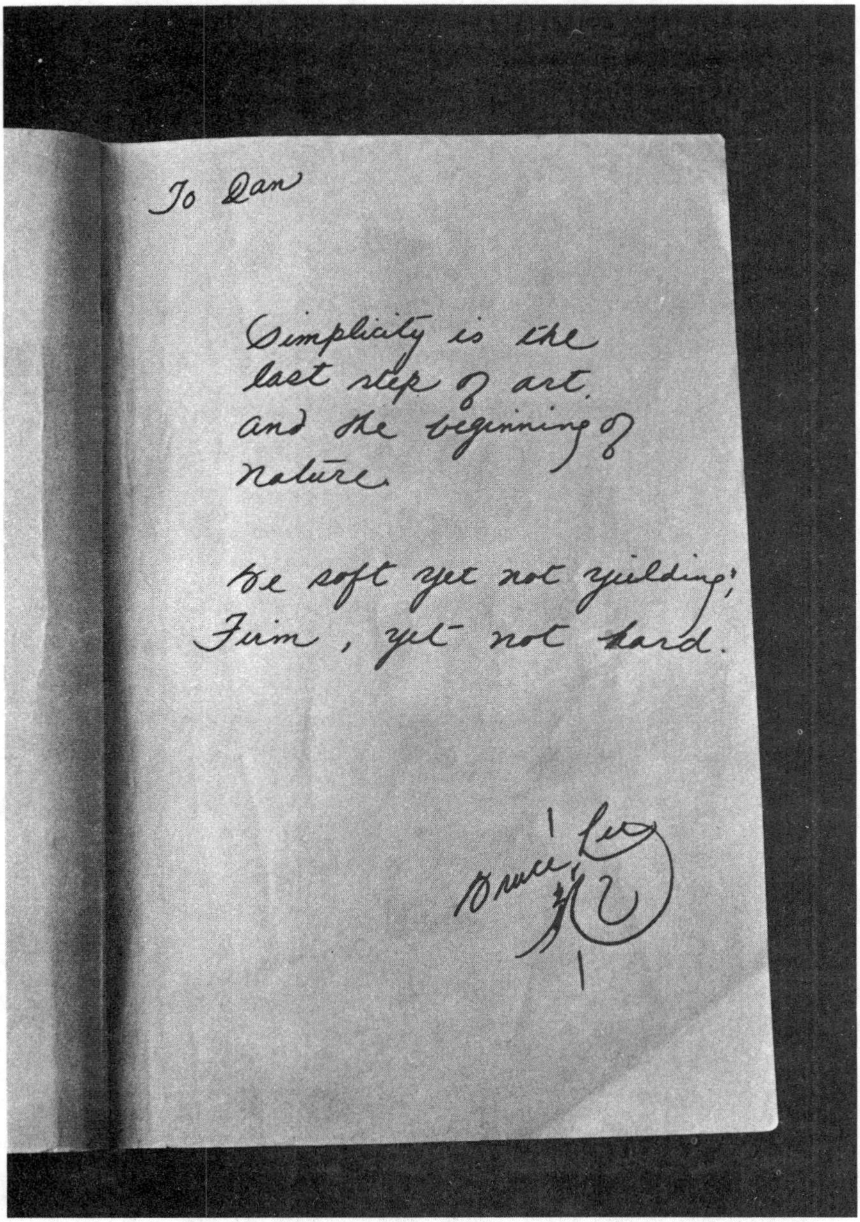

To Dan

Simplicity is the
last step of art.
And the beginning of
nature.

Be soft yet not yielding;
Firm, yet not hard.

Bruce Lee

Some instructors of martial arts favor forms, the more complex and fancy the better. Some, on the other hand, are obsessed with super mental power (like Captain Marvel or Superman). Still some favor deformed hands and legs, and devote their time on fighting bricks, stones, boards, etc., etc.

To me the extradordinary aspect of martial arts lies in its simplicity. Martial arts is simply the 'direct expression' of one's feeling with the minimum of movements and energy. Every movement is being so of itself without the artificialities which people tend to complicate it. The easy way is always the right way, and martial arts is nothing at all special; the closer to the true way of martial arts, the less wastage of expression there is.

Instead of facing combat in its suchness, quite a few systems of martial arts accumulate 'fancyness' that distort and cramp their practitioners and distract them from the actual reality of combat, which is 'simple' and 'direct' and 'non-classical'. Instead of going immediately to the heart of things, flowery forms and artificial techniques (organized despair!) are 'ritually practiced' to simulate actual combat. Thus, instead of 'being' in combat, these practitioners are idealistically 'doing' something about combat. Worse still, super mental this and spiritual that are ignorantly incorporated until these practitioners are drifting further and further into the distance of abstraction and mystery that what they do resemble anything from acrobatics to modern dancing but the actual reality of combat.

All these complexness are actually futile attempts to 'arrest' and 'fix' the ever changing movements in combat and to dissect and analyse them like a corpse. Real combat is not fixed and is very much 'alive'. Such means of practice (a form of paralysis) will only 'solidify' and 'condition' what was once fluid and alive. When

*you get off sophistication and what not and look at it 'realistically',
these robots (practitioners that is) are blindly devoting to the
systematic uselessness of practicing 'routines' or 'stunts' that lead
to nowhere.*

*Martial arts is to be looked through without fancy suits and
matching ties, and it will remain a secret when we anxiously
look for sophistication and deadly techniques. If there are really any
secrets at all, they must have been missed by the seeking and striving
of its practitioners (after all, how many ways are there to come in on
an opponent without 'deviating too much from the natural course'?).
True martial arts values the wonder of the ordinary and the cultivation
of martial arts is not daily increase, but daily decrease. Being wise in
the martial arts does not mean adding more, but to do away
with ornamentation and be simply simple-----like a sculptor building
a statue not by adding but by hacking away the unessential so that
the truth will be revealed unobstructed. In short, martial arts is
satisfied with one's bare hand without the fancy decoration of colorful gloves which tend to hinder the natural function of the hand.*

*Art is the expression of the self. The more complicated and
restrictive a method is, the lesser the opportunity for the expression
of one's original sense of freedom! The techniques, though they
play an important role in the early stage, should not be too restrictive,
complex or mechanical. If we cling to them we will become bound by
their limitation. Remember, YOU are 'expressing' the technique and
not 'doing' the technique number two, stance two, section four?
like sound and echo without any deliberation. It is as though when
I call you, you answer me or when I throw something to you, you catch
it, that's all.*

−BRUCE LEE 1965

49

By 1967 Bruce Lee had officially opened his third—and his last—martial arts *kwoon*. He chose to set up shop on the bottom floor of an innocuous-looking, two-story edifice adjacent to Los Angeles' Old Chinatown. Like its forerunners in Seattle and Oakland, the nondescript, grey-brick structure bore no identifying marks or sign whatsoever, and its windows were painted over with red enamel to ensure total anonymity. Thus to the casual passerby sauntering down College Street there appeared to be nothing out of the ordinary about number 628. Indeed, a majority of the traffic to and fro consisted of befuddled baseball fans that had lost their way while headed for Dodger Stadium, a few blocks away. On Bruce's orders absolutely no visitors were allowed inside Jun Fan Institute number three, and he purposely limited enrollment to a select cadre of extremely talented martial artists and a few "high rollers" he knew in the entertainment industry.

Bruce hated big classes. He felt that the only way to maintain the quality of instruction was to teach each student on a one-to-one basis. And he was right. Take, for instance, a guy who trains boxers. He can train two, maybe three, but that's it. This is because he has to know his fighters inside and out: Does the man have any emotional hang-ups? Does he get all tensed up before a fight? Is he easily excitable? Is he nervous? Is he lethargic? And if so, what steps can be taken to get him into the proper frame of mind? In other words, each individual has his own unique personality traits that effect his performance—and each one has to be handled in a different way. Which is why Bruce positively rejected any and all offers to establish a franchise network across the country of Kato's Gung-Fu schools.

In the interest of preserving historical accuracy, I should perhaps interject here that we had in fact opened a semi-public school earlier in 1966. It was located directly behind Wayne Chan's pharmacy in the heart of Chinatown, in a room that has since been converted into a movie theater. In addition, although as then Bruce had not yet come up with the term Jeet Kune Do—and by that I mean the underlying principles—he had already scrapped his modified Wing Chun

In reminiscing about my training with Bruce I revisited the various locations where we worked out together.

I was amazed when I went to look for Bruce Lee's first apartment in Westwood. It has been replaced by a giant building used for parking cars. It was here that Bruce first trained me when he moved to Los Angeles.

This is Barrington Plaza in West Los Angeles, another training site for my lessons. We trained in the living room of this apartment.

Bruce also trained me in back of Wayne Chan's pharmacy in China-town. Bruce worked with only three of us here: Wayne Chan, Tony Hum and myself.

style, which I felt was really good. I still think it was pretty good because it contained a lot of truth. But it was obvious that he was progressing.

Daniel Lee, an electrical engineer and Chinese language instructor, was the first student admitted to the Chinatown *kwoon.* Thinking back on the early days in Los Angeles, Dan remembers that "this was the time when Bruce was uncommitted to the movies or television. He had more time to train us, and he maintained such high standards for our training that he also gave everyone a specially prescribed supplementary fitness program. He'd look at you and say, you've got to work on this area, that area, stretching, and so on. He really meant business and he worked very hard—four times a week. That's dedication."

Inspired by Bruce's example, those of us who studied under him still stand in awe of his greatness. "He was probably the one person I respected most," says Dan Lee of his mentor. "Bruce Lee was a very straightforward person—very straightforward, very intense, but most of all, very honest. If he liked you, he liked you. He didn't hold back any punches;

628 College Street, Chinatown, Los Angeles,
was the start of the Jun Fan Gung Fu Institute.

The third place Bruce moved to, in
Inglewood, California. We trained
here as well as at the Chinatown Gym.

if he didn't like you, he said so . . . and that's the kind of person you like because you know he's going to say exactly the same thing behind your back as he would to your face."

This same integrity that Bruce Lee lived by also guides the principles of his fighting art—Jeet Kune Do. In the same way that Bruce would never think of applying fixed formulas or ideas to his approach to life, the principles of JKD depend upon total freedom.

Developing from Bruce's firm conviction that actual combat rarely, if ever, conformed to the dogmatic do's and don'ts of systematized styles—JKD's only bounds and limits exist in the individual abilities of the practitioners. It is an art where the only rule is that there are no rules. We see, then, that by removing the constraints of set patterns and responses, a freedom to flow naturally with reality comes about. And the closer you get to reality, the less you need complicated devices or techniques as crutches.

As human beings we have a tendency to be partial to that which we do best; something in our physical or psychological makeup, that is, causes us to favor the tried and true at the

Bruce and Linda moved from there to Culver City, and of course this became another training site. This is the back of Bruce's patio at his Culver City house where Kareem Abdul Jabbar met him. Bruce told me that Kareem could kick the top of this basketball rim.

The fifth and final move of the Lee family in the Los Angeles area was to this house in Bel Air.

He used to train a small group in his backyard in Bel Air. Kareem Abdul Jabar once placed my daughter up on this roof.

In 1970 Bruce Lee told me to abandon and close the Chinatown Gym, and take a small select group to my house to train. I lived then on east Fernrock Street in Carson, California. We trained in my garage and sometimes in my backyard. Bruce abandoned all the organized schools of Jeet Kune Do because he felt it was too easy for the students to mistake the agenda as The Truth and to take the class program as The Way.

It was too small and too confined in my garage. With the help of Alfred Haber, a close friend and student, and Richard Lee, a student who was also an architect and designer by profession, we built a small 30' x 40' gym in my backyard.

When Bruce died on July 20, 1973, we were still training in this little gym in my backyard. In December of 1974 my family and I moved to Harbor City, California. My backyard in Harbor City was not large enough to set up a gym. We had loads of equipment and no place to put it.

In April 1974, we decided to open a school because we wanted Jeet Kune Do to continue to flourish. Yet we all knew that Bruce never wanted us to teach commercially under the name of Jeet Kune Do. We decided to kill two birds with one stone, so we named our school the Filipino Kali Academy. There were ten classes at the academy, but only one in Jeet Kune Do, and it's still that way today. The rest of the classes promote the Filipino arts of Kali, Escrima, Sikaran, Dumog, Panantukan, Silat, Kuntao, and a combination of Western boxing, kick boxing, and Wing Chun.

The students go through 3 phases at the academy before they are voted into the Jeet Kune Do class by the rest of the members.

The site of the school is 23018 S. Normandie, Torrance, California.

55

exclusion of the unfamiliar or unknown. Let me use myself, for example: because of my height, 5'5½", I don't feel that comfortable in the kicking range. Even though I can kick over my head, it means hitting most people in the chest—maybe even the waist! Instead, I like to use a lot of rapid hand strikes and trapping—and lot of rapid low kicks because that's me. And since I feel insecure in the grappling range, I stay away from it, and guard that range with great care. So the fact is, we derive a certain sense of well-being from sticking to the familiar—which, according to Bruce, is the first disease of the mind.

Therefore, he used to refer to JKD's structure as being "a circle with no circumference." The idea is not to attach yourself to any one thing. Don't hesitate to draw from everything around you: boxing, fencing, wrestling, karate, judo, ballet, modern dance, etc., or anything that can be applied from any field—even biting and clawing, for that matter. Then, finally, know your strengths, your weaknesses too, and be able to recognize your opponent's strong points and weak points—avoiding the former and exploiting the latter.

Bruce was quick to point out that Jeet Kune Do is more than simply a composite of many different styles and systems. It has a definite central theme—preserving the centerline, a constant rhythmic flow and the ability to "fit in" to the opponent's techniques—that must be observed at all times. And although the art encompasses many things as we have seen, there is always something to be added, but not in helter-skelter fashion because the main purpose is the preservation of the common thread that binds it all together.

This fitting in spirit, which is the essence of Jeet Kune Do, Bruce discovered many years ago while sailing alone in a junk. Frustrated that he had been unable to master the art of gentle detachment, which is being able to neutralize an opponent's effort at the same time minimizing the expenditure of one's own energy, he was taking a week off from practice at Yip Man's suggestion to "think about it." As his frustration began to approach its zenith, suddenly the thought struck him that the very substance which kept him afloat—water—was the embodiment of the ethereal spirit of the martial arts.

After all, one could strike it and nothing happened. Or one could stab it, and it suffered no dent. And to grasp a handful of it was impossible. Furthermore, water automatically assumed the shape of its container, and though it appeared weak, it could in time penetrate any substance on earth. Thus in the nature of water Bruce had discovered the guiding principle of Jeet Kune Do.

As has been said many times, the keynote of Jeet Kune Do is simplicity. The movements are crisp and efficient, utilizing the most direct lines and angles. Finally, it is non-classical, eschewing the usually passive blocking tactics. For in Bruce's opinion, efficiency meant anything that scores.

Getting back to what it was like learning from Bruce: Our training was both physical and psychological. He taught us to be mentally prepared for combat; that was his big thing—the proper mental attitude. He wanted us to form a high opinion of ourselves. And then he would tear us down so that we wouldn't become complacent.

It was Bruce's belief that in learning a martial art one passed through three stages of development, and the Chinatown program revolved around these stages. The first stage is the "Primitive Stage." It is the stage of ORIGINAL ignorance in which a person knows nothing of the art of combat. In a fight he "simply" blocks and strikes instinctively without a concern as to what is being right and wrong. Of course, he might not be so-called scientific but he is nevertheless BEING HIMSELF and his attack or defense is fluid.

The second stage, the stage of sophistication, begins when a person starts his training. He is taught the different ways of blocking and striking, and various ways of kicking, of standing, of breathing, thinking . . . unquestionably he has gained a scientific knowledge of combat, but unfortunately, his original self and sense of freedom are lost and his action no longer flows by itself. His mind tends to freeze at different movements for calculation and analysis; even worse, he might be "INTELLECTUALLY BOUND" and maintaining himself OUTSIDE the actual reality.

The third stage, the stage of artlessness, occurs when, after years of serious and hard practice, he realizes that after all

If nothing within you stays rigid, Outward things will disclose themselves. Moving, be like water. Still, be like a mirror. Respond like an echo.

Nothingness cannot be confined, the softest thing cannot be snapped.

Be like water making its way through cracks. Do not be assertive, but adjust ourselves to the object, we shall find The Way round or through it. The softer (pliable) a substance is, the narrower the crack through which it can pass.

Gung-Fu is nothing special and instead of trying to impose his mind, he adjusts himself to the opponent like water pressing on an earthen wall—it flows through the slightest cracks. There is nothing to "try" to do but be purposeless and formless like water. All his "classical" techniques and standard style are minimized (if not wiped out) and nothingness prevails; he is no longer CONFINED.

In the introduction to his early book titled *Chinese Gung-Fu: The Philosophical Art of Self-Defense,* Bruce wrote: "It is true that the mental aspect of Gung-Fu is the desired end; however in order to achieve this stage, technical skill has to come first." What Bruce was saying here I, in turn, have come to describe as *totality of being and constant growth.* Let me explain briefly:

As I have said before, Bruce did not look upon Jeet Kune Do as an end in itself; rather it was a means of promoting spiritual awareness through a physical art. Through continual striving and achieving, exceeding certain goals and falling short of others, experiencing the perpetual ups and downs of this essentially bodily endeavor—you begin to see that there is indeed a limitation to physical achievement. Lack of ambition occurs, lifestyles change, old age sets in—whatever. At that point you can either give up entirely and become stagnant, or begin exploring in other directions. But, you might ask, what is left to explore? Simple: the mind or the inner self. Along these lines Bruce was fond of quoting Charles P. Steinmetz, the late electronics genius, who shortly before his death in 1923 was asked what branch of science would make the most progress in the next twenty-five years. After pausing for several minutes to think, he replied in a flash: "Spiritual realization."

Bruce was twenty-six when he opened the Los Angeles *kwoon,* also a student of Kung-Fu for fully half his life. Although he was still a young man in comparison to others worthy of the title "master," he had by then attained such an uncommon level of proficiency that he was virtually untouchable; very few people were capable of giving him a meaningful workout. As I have mentioned, too, he had already authored a most unique martial arts text, which

Bruce giving a lecture at the
Chinatown Gym in 1967.

A sign that hangs in the Filipino Kali Academy that was originally at James Lee's school in Oakland.

A picture of me taken by the
Haber brothers in 1967 with
the original Jun Fan Gung-Fu
banner in the Chinatown gym.

A Zen saying that hangs at the
Filipino Kali Academy.

showed that he was well versed in the philosophies behind the arts. So when it came time for him to pass his ideas along to others, he certainly had no misgivings about his ability to do it well. He was good and he knew it. Therefore he gleefully thumbed his nose at tradition; cast the proverbial "book" out the window, and in the meantime revolutionized the martial arts—catapulting them into worldly prominence.

I have said many times that what struck me most about Bruce as an instructor was how he remained completely at ease, constantly making jokes and keeping a relaxed atmosphere yet still maintaining discipline. Jerry Poteet, another one of the early students at College Street, remembers that Bruce could be a strict disciplinarian when the situation called for it.

"One time he [Bruce] got up in front of class and said, 'I know that *socially* a lot of us in here are friends, and outside the school I'm Bruce. But in here you call me *sifu*. Because of the informality, there has to be some discipline. If this school was in China, there would be a lot of people here now missing their front teeth.' "

By the same token, Bruce could be very compassionate and understanding. For example, I remember an episode that happened when we were practicing this rather difficult kicking exercise. There was one guy in the class who was particularly clumsy and having a difficult time of it. Truthfully, he looked really terrible; and one of the other students started laughing. Bruce just looked over at him and said, "If you can do better, come up here right now. Or else, wipe that smile off your face and I want it silent from now on." As talented as he was, Bruce always respected you for your ability.

Jerry Poteet adds: "At one point I was short of money and felt badly because I couldn't pay. Then Bruce wrote me a letter saying, 'Come on in. Forget all about it until you can. You're sincere, that's what counts.' "

Whenever we trained the emphasis was on conditioning. In addition to the usual physical fitness exercises, there was "awareness" and "tool" training as well. The goal of awareness training was to sharpen our sense of perception so that we could recognize, identify and react to an opponent's

I demonstrate the finger-jab
and Bruce explains the finer
points in this picture, taken
in 1967.

An aluminum emblem made
by George Lee for Bruce at
the Filipino Kali Academy.

Bruce demonstrates the art of
trapping with Tony Hum as
students Phil Bardelli and
Daniel Lee watch.

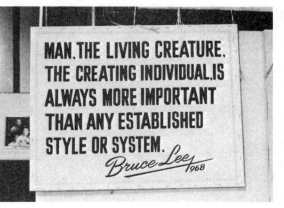

MAN. THE LIVING CREATURE.
THE CREATING INDIVIDUAL, IS
ALWAYS MORE IMPORTANT
THAN ANY ESTABLISHED
STYLE OR SYSTEM.
Bruce Lee 1968

A saying of Bruce's that hangs
at the Filipino Kali Academy.

moves instantaneously without thinking or being bound by what Bruce termed "psychical stoppage." By not focusing on any one single object, the mind is freed to concentrate on the here and now. This type of concentration is best illustrated by the audience at a football game; instead of giving attention merely to the player with the ball, the spectators take in the entire playing field at once. In a similar way, concentration in Jeet Kune Do means not dwelling on any particular aspect of the opponent. Ultimately, the mind wills and the body obeys.

Bruce took a fascination in developing a wide variety of training aids and equipment upon which to sharpen his combat tools—feet and hands. Besides availing himself of the heavy bag and speed bag familiar to boxers, he introduced the top-and-bottom bag, which is suspended from the floor and ceiling so that it would return in a totally unpredictable manner. While the heavy bag and speed bag were used to develop power, coordination and reflexes, the top-and-bottom bag was used to perfect his timing. Also, there was the padded focus glove which a training partner could wave at every conceivable angle so that Bruce could practice correct distancing—that is, the punch or kick arriving on target with maximum force and extension.

Most classical Kung-Fu systems require that the novice spend anywhere from the first six months to a year poised in the rudimentary stances or "horses." This is supposedly necessary in order to build strength in the legs, instill patience and test the student's sincerity. Beyond this, their practical application remains the topic of much debate.

Bruce called such ancient rituals "exercises in futility." He also took exception to those instructors who tried to "teach swimming on dry land," to revive another one of his favorite phrases. He insisted that without delay, from the earliest beginnings, students must be taught to spar effectively so as to greatly increase their chances for survival in the streets.

According to Bruce: "In sparring you should wear suitable protective equipment and go all-out. Then you can truly learn the correct timing and distance for the delivery of kicks, punches, etc. It's a good idea to spar with all kinds of individuals—tall, short, fast, clumsy—yes, at times a clumsy fellow will mess up a better man because his awkwardness serves as a sort of broken rhythm."

Dan Lee agrees that most martial artists would do themselves good to incorporate more realistic conditions into their training. "You put on the body protectors," he says, "and go all-out. That's the only way. When it's going to be all-out, your frame of mind changes because you know if you make one mistake, he's coming right at you. And then you really begin to respect his punch as the real thing."

Emphasizing large doses of almost-real combat to teach calm and quick reaction under pressure, JKD is most effective in actual use. In the advanced practitioners, punches and other attacks become reflex actions, guided solely by senses heightened through countless hours of actual sparring. . . . The instant an opening occurs, the attack is already on the way. Because of the simplicity of the techniques, the attack is extremely powerful and effective.

Yet, beyond the techniques and their infinite variations and applications, the spirit with which they are delivered is equally—if not more—important. For instance: The secret of kicking, as Bruce taught it, was controlled anger. I remember once he asked me to throw a sidekick. He held this shield for about five minutes, and I kicked at it with what I thought was everything I had. But Bruce wasn't satisfied. "You're posing," he said. "Think of something you hate." I kicked it again, but the results were the same. Finally, he walked over nonchalantly and slapped me on the face. For a second I forgot he was Bruce Lee and I came toward him. He laughed. "OK, *now* kick. That's what I want."

From a combat standpoint, Bruce felt that most classical styles were unrealistic because they placed equal importance on form as well as efficiency. It was necessary, he said, to constantly break tradition in order to improve. To him the main concern should not be how good some particular form of combat looked, but how good it worked. Being a PE teacher, I can see that this is what in fact has happened in nearly every sport.

A decisive leap. In your case it was the side kick that caused you to lose your 'presence of the primordial state.' However, today your side kick became a tool to unlock a spiritual goal. There was spiritual loosening along with physical loosening, a sort of unconcerned immersion in oneself. The original sense of freedom was there. Congratulations! The side kick took the place of the ego.

—A personal note discovered in Bruce Lee's note book.

Take, for example, the mile run. Until Roger Banister broke that mythical human barrier, the four-minute mile was thought to be beyond man's capabilities. Since he broke tradition, the world knows it can be done and a score of others have achieved that goal.

The accepted standard for the shot-put was to face sideways toward the officials and heave that sixteen-pound steel ball for all you were worth; in other words, all strength and little technique. And then along came Perry O'Brien. Instead of facing the officials, he turned completely around, went into a semi-crouch position, kicked one leg high in the air, spun around after a couple of short strides letting his momentum do most of the work and presto!—a new world's record. And also a new standard method of shot-putting. That standard is again being changed today by a man named Brian Oldfield, who uses a "discus method" of putting the shot.

Or take basketball. Until little Hank Luisetti arrived on the scene and began pumping in one-hand jumpers like crazy from the outside, the two-hand set-shot was the only way to go. The critics said Luisetti's style would never work because it left the shooter off balance, he had no control over the ball, etc. But when was the last time you saw a two-hand set-shot in the NBA?

For centuries man has been jumping over obstacles. In 1887 the standard or classical method of high jumping was called the "scissor style." In 1895 Mike Sweeney broke tradition and the world's record by using the "Eastern roll." This became the accepted or standard way of high jumping. In 1912 George Horine broke tradition and the record by using a style called the "Western roll." This became the model and the way to high jump. In 1936 Dave Albritton established another way called the "straddle style" of high jumping. Recently a man named Fosbury, who the coaches thought was crazy, decided to go over backwards. . . . Need I say more?

Finally, let me say that it is impossible to overemphasize the importance of Bruce's stay in the Los Angeles area. He felt that he really reached his plateau down here because the city was a hotbed of martial arts activity in the late Sixties and early Seventies. This gave him an opportunity to meet and work out with most of the big-name tournament karate fighters—among them Chuck Norris, Joe Lewis, Mike Stone and Bob Wall—which meant that he was exposed to virtually every style and system under the sun.

In truth, a lot of the experts Bruce sparred with—including some national karate champions who were well known throughout the country—came away convinced that he had supernatural powers. Louis Delgado, for one, once described Bruce as "quite baffling—almost as though he had ESP." Yet Bruce himself always pooh-poohed such nonsense. He used to explain to us that his unreal demonstrations of power and quickness were merely the result of proper muscle groupings —and relaxation.

A lot of people think that JKD is something metaphysical, but it's not. Really it's quite simple. Basically, I think what it boils down to is this: JKD is Bruce Lee's philosophy, based on things he observed to be true.

Today, 628 College Street houses a sewing factory. The windows are no longer obliterated by red paint, and the interior is clearly visible—with nary a trace remaining of its former tenants. Gone, too, is the miniature tombstone that once stood by the door and greeted students with the now famous inscription: "In memory of a once fluid man, crammed and distorted by the classical mess."

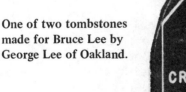

One of two tombstones made for Bruce Lee by George Lee of Oakland.

IN MEMORY
OF
A ONCE FLUID MAN
CRAMMED AND DISTORTED
BY
THE CLASSICAL MESS

截拳道 **Jeet Kune Do**

HOW "JEET KUNE DO" WAS COINED

It all began in the early part of 1968 while Bruce and I were driving along in the car. We were talking about fencing, Western fencing. Bruce said the most efficient means of countering in fencing was the *stop-hit*. A stop-hit is when you do not parry and then counter, it's all done in one step. When the opponent attacks, you intercept his move with a thrust or hit of your own. It is designed to score a hit in the midst of the attacker's action, and is the highest and most economical of all the counters.

Then Bruce said, "We should call our method the 'stop-hitting fist style', or the 'intercepting fist style'."

"What would that be in Chinese?" I asked.

"That would be Jeet Kune Do," he said.

Jeet Kune Do means the way of the stopping fist, or the way of the intercepting fist. So, instead of blocking and then hitting, our main concept is to dispense with blocking completely, and instead to intercept and hit. We realize that this cannot be done all the time, but this is the main theme.

Up until 1967 our method was called "Jun Fan" Gung Fu, which was a modification of various techniques from Northern Praying Mantis, Southern Praying Mantis, Choy Li Fut, Eagle Claw, Western Boxing, Hung Gar, Thai Boxing, wrestling, Judo, Jiu Jitsu and several Northern Gung-Fu styles. It is obvious that Wing Chun was the main nucleus and all the other methods evolved around it.

It was during this time that Bruce developed his own particular style of kicking, modified from the Northern styles of Gung Fu, and greatly improved by the way he trained for it.

In later years he became sorry that he ever coined the term Jeet Kune Do because he felt that it, too, was limiting, and according to Bruce, "There is no such thing as a style if you totally understand the roots of combat."

The term "JKD" came about naturally, because Bruce used to abbreviate much of his material, such as "HIA," "ABC," "ABD," "SAA," "PIA."

One day I said to him, "This JKD is fantastic," and he said, "Hey, I like that term JKD," and he used it as a shortcut for Jeet Kune Do. In our personal conversations, we used "JKD" as a term for something very good, out of this world, unique, or very fast.

So, for instance, we could be driving along and see a restaurant we liked, and say,

"Yeah, the food at that place is JKD!"

Or,

"That movie I saw last night was JKD!"

Or,

"Mmmmm, his singing is JKD."

Or,

"Wow, that painting is JKD!"

However, Bruce also said, "JKD is just a name, don't fuss over it."

An Explaination of the JKD Emblem

Using No Way
As Way
Having No Limitation
As Limitation

Instead of opposing force by force, a JKD man completes his opponent's movement by 'accepting' his flow of energy as he aims it, and defeats him by 'borrowing' his own force. In order to reconcile oneself to the changing movements of the opponent, a JKD man should first of all understand the true meaning of Yin/Yang, the basic structure of JKD.

JKD is based on the symbol of the Yin and Yang, a pair of mutually complementary and interdependent forces that act continuously, without cessation, in this universe. In the above symbol, the Yin and Yang are two interlocking parts of 'one whole', each containing within its confines the qualities of its complementaries. Etymologically the characters of Yin and Yang mean darkness and light. The ancient character of Yin, the dark part of the circle, is a drawing of clouds and hill. Yin can represent anything in the universe as: negativeness, passiveness, gentleness, internal, insubstantiality, femaleness, moon, darkness, night, etc. The other complementary half of the circle is Yang, which in its ancient form is anything as positiveness, activeness, firmness, external, substantiality, maleness, sun, brightness, day, etc.

The common mistake of most martial artists is to identify these two forces, Yin and Yang, as dualistic (thus the so called soft style and the firm style). Yin/Yang is one inseparate force of one unceasing interplay of movement. They are conceived of as essentially one, or as two co-existing forces of one indivisible whole. They are neither cause and effect, but should be looked at as sound and echo, or light and shadow. If this 'oneness' is viewed as two separate entities, realization of the ultimate reality of JKD won't be achieved. In reality things are 'whole' and can not be separated into two parts. When I say the heat makes me perspire, the heat and perspiring are just one process as they are co-existent and the one could not exist but for the other. If a person riding a bicycle wishes to go somewhere, he cannot pump on both the pedals at the same time. In order to go forward, he has to pump on one pedal and release the other. So the movement of going forward requires this 'oneness' of pumping and releasing. Pumping is the result of releasing and vice versa, each being the cause and result of the other. Things do have their complementaries, and complementaries co-exist. Instead of mutually exclusive, they are mutually dependent and are a function each of the other.

In the Yin/Yang symbol there is a white spot on the black part and a black spot on the white one. This is to illustrate the balance in life, for nothing can survive long by going to either extremes, be it pure Yin (gentleness) or pure Yang (firmness). Notice that the stiffest tree is most easily cracked, while the bamboo or willow survive by bending with the wind. In JKD, Yang (firmness) should be concealed in Yin (gentleness) and Yin in Yang. Thus a JKD man should be soft yet not laxed, firm, yet not hard.

FIRMNESS/GENTLENESS

What is gentleness? It is a pliable reed in the wind----it neither opposes nor gives way.

What is the highest state of yielding? It is like clutching water.

What is true stillness? Stillness in movement.

What is adaptation? It is like the immediacy of the shadow adjusting itself to the moving body.

You wish to know what is internal school and external school? Not two!

–BRUCE LEE

This emblem is at the Filipino Kali Academy in Torrance, California. It represents the spirit of the dragon. Bruce thought of it as being too ornamental and classical.

Bruce giving a lecture at the old Chinatown Gym, 1967.

Another emblem with philosopy from the Filipino Kali Academy. The scroll explains about Bruce Lee's accomplishments in life. It was draped over his casket at the Seattle Funeral.

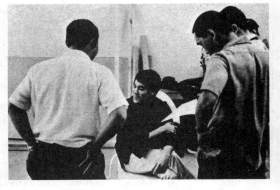

Bruce Lee talking with students at the old Chinatown Gym in 1967. His classes were always informal but dynamic.

Bruce and I discuss policies of the Chinatown Gym, 1967.

One of Bruce's sayings in the Filipino Kali Academy.

MY FOLLOWERS IN JEET KUNE DO. DO LISTEN TO THIS... ALL FIXED SET PATTERN ARE INCAPABLE OF ADAPTABILITY OR PLIABILITY. THE TRUTH IS OUTSIDE OF ALL FIXED PATTERNS.

Bruce Lee 1966

Original drawings by Bruce from his first book.

Ted remembers that Bruce was very meticulous in whatever he did. In photo sessions, he actually became the photographer to make sure everything was correct to the smallest detail.

Ted Wong was one of Bruce Lee's closest friends in the Los Angeles area. He was one of the few non-martial artists Bruce trained. You could say he trained Ted from scratch.

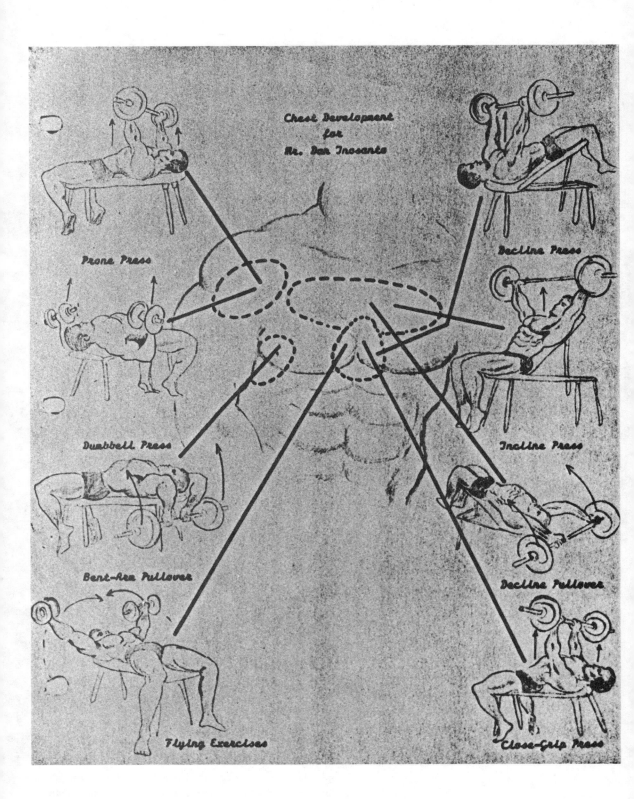

Chest Development
for
Mr. Don Inosanto

Prone Press

Decline Press

Dumbbell Press

Incline Press

Bent-Arm Pullover

Decline Pullover

Flying Exercises

Close-Grip Press

One of the reasons Bruce wanted to teach only three to five students at one time was because he wanted to specialize in each individual. In other words, he wanted to develop the complete individual, emotionally and mentally as well as physically.

Bruce gave a different program to each student, and would periodically change it as they progressed. Some received flexibility programs because they were too tight. Others got coordination programs, agility programs, strength and power programs, or physical development programs, depending on what they needed.

This is just one of the programs he made for me.

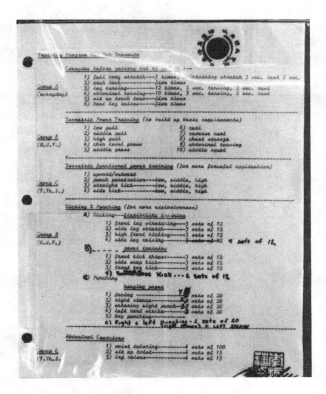

Bruce gave me this program in 1967. He changed it every three to six months to fit my needs. With large classes, he would never have been able to go into this kind of detail with a student.

These are membership cards used by Bruce Lee for the three branches of the Jun Fan Gung Fu Institute. There were eight ranks in the Jun Fan Gung Fu Institute. This ranking system was replaced by a newer ranking system, then ranking systems altogether were abandoned by Bruce because he felt ranking was unimportant.

One of Bruce Lee's business cards.

A rare photo of Bruce Lee and James Lee taken in front of the College Street school.

Bruce Lee, Allen Joe and myself eating at a Chinese restaurant in 1967 for one of the many get-togethers with the Oakland bunch in L.A.

This membership card was once used by the Jun Fan Gung Fu Institute. It is no longer used by the Jeet Kune Do Organization.

Bruce's personal stationery, one of his business cards and a symbol pin he gave to his students. He always went first class. All his printed matter was colorful and on expensive paper.

Before I studied the art, a punch to me is just like a punch, a kick just like a kick. After I've studied the art, a punch is no longer a punch, a kick no longer a kick. Now that I understood the art, a punch is just like a punch, a kick just like a kick.

There is nothing much in this art. Take things as they are. Punch when you have to punch. Kick when you have to kick.

Not being tense but ready, not thinking but not dreaming, not being set but flexible----It is being 'wholly' and quietly 'alive', aware and alert, ready for whatever may come.

The height of cultivation runs to simplicity. Half-way cultivation runs to ornamentation.

It's not daily increase but daily decrease----hack away the unessential!

Would that we could at once strike with the eyes!----In the long way from the eye through the arm to the fist, how much is lost!

Please do not disregard your five natural senses to rely on a so called "sixth"!

I'm moving and not moving at all. I'm like the moon underneath the waves that ever go on rolling and rocking.

Give up thinking as though not giving it up. Observe the techniques as though not observing.

To change with change is the changeless state.

The stillness in stillness is not the real stillness, only when there is stillness in movement does the universal rhythm manifest.

Nothingness cannot be confined; the softest thing cannot be snapped.

–BRUCE LEE

Oyster beef, beef rice and root beer were Bruce Lee's favorite foods.

Martial art styles are like food. A true connoisseur should partake of all types. If you are Japanese and you only want to study and believe in the Japanese method of martial art, you are missing the boat. If you are Chinese and you only want to study Chinese martial art, you are missing the boat. If you are Korean and only want to study Korean martial art, if you are Filipino and you only want to study Filipino martial art, if you are Okinawan and you only want to study Okinawan styles, you are missing the boat. If you are American or European and you only want to study boxing, fencing or wrestling, you are missing the boat. And if you only try to "Americanize" the Oriental arts, you are missing the boat. It is my belief that a martial artist should not be bound to one thing. If you only eat oyster beef and root beer, you are missing the boat.

I am Filipino with a little Spanish and Chinese, but I do not limit myself to Chinese, Spanish and Filipino food. I eat Mexican food, Italian food, French food, German food, Greek food, Armenian food, Japanese food, Korean, Indonesian and Thai food, Middle-Eastern food, Chinese food—any type of food that tastes good. I have to try them to find out if I like them.

Although I am primarily Filipino, I can honestly say that there are many Filipino dishes that I dislike, and many Filipino foods that I greatly enjoy. This is true about Filipino martial arts. There are many things I like about them, and there are a few things I dislike about them. Bruce once told me, "Be proud that you are a Filipino, and be proud of their martial arts, but don't be bound to them just because you are a Filipino. Experience the beauty of each. Know its strong points and its weak points. It is obvious that no race, nation style or organization can claim a monopoly on all the things that are good, or for that matter, all the things that are bad."

To quote a Zen saying, "In the landscape of spring, the flowering buds grow, some short and some long."

We found this certificate intended for Steve McQueen while going through some of Bruce's notes.

BRUCE LEE'S
TAO OF
CHINESE GUNG FU
振藩拳道

以無限為有限

以無法為有法

學生 McQueen 係 Calif. 省 Los Angeles 縣人在館修練期滿准予升入第一級

此證

李振藩

一九六七年九月 日

Date Sept. 1967

This is to certify that

Steve McQueen

Is personally taught by Bruce Lee, and having fulfilled the necessary requirements, is hereby promoted to 1st. rank in Bruce Lee's Tao of Chinese Gung Fu.

BRUCE LEE

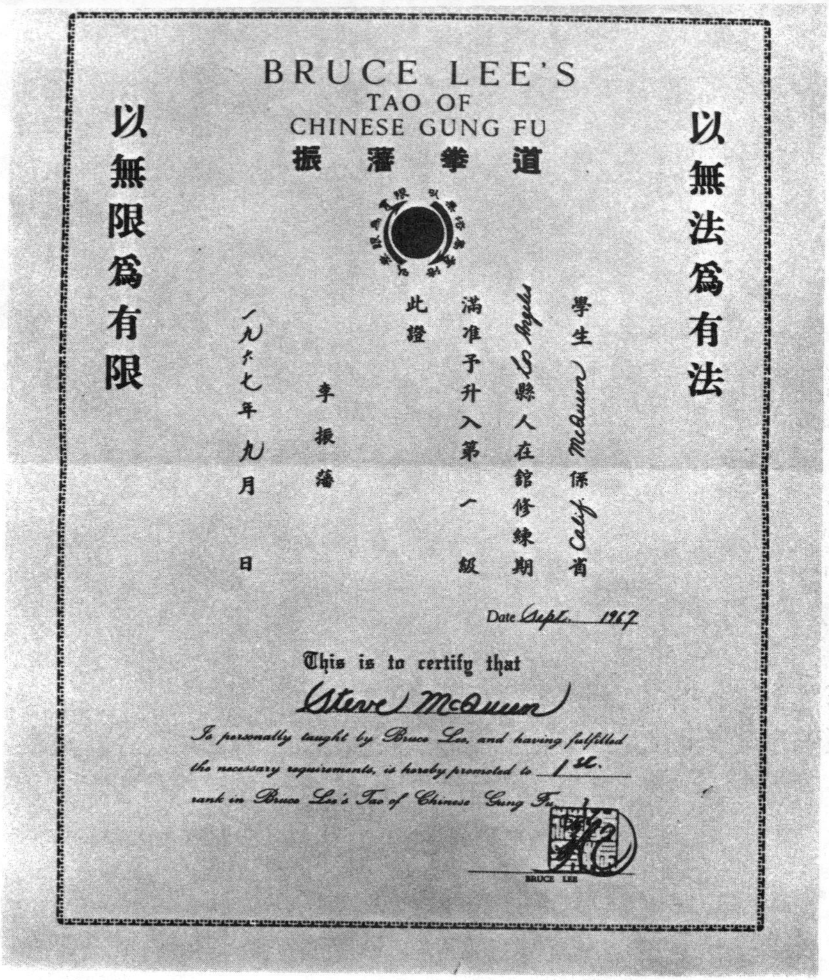

This letter, along with the encouragement of Richard Bustillo, Daniel Lee and Jerry Poteet were the main factors that convinced me to preserve and perpetuate Bruce Lee's art of Jeet Kune Do.

Dear Dan,

I have not talked with you for a long time, hope everything is OK.

I know it was a great shock at Bruce's death, with all the emotion that goes with the passing of a friend.

I've sort of heard by the grape vine that you took it very hard. One thing that Bruce would have wanted is for everybody to do their thing, and be happy. I do not think it is commercializing yourself to do your thing, as Bruce was doing his thing.

You're a good man, live your life the fullest.

I remain,

Sincerely,

Steve McQueen

Steve McQueen

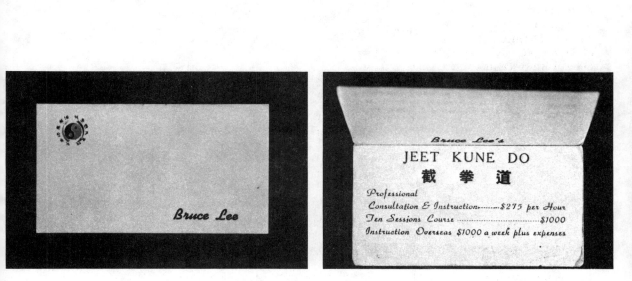

This business card was the first publication of his professional
fees. To his close friends, however, he never charged a cent.

I gave this plaque to Bruce on his birthday from the senior
students at the L.A. Branch in Chinatown. It was one of
the few awards he cherished. His many trophies were
discarded.

In the beginning we used to dress in traditional classical Gung-Fu uniforms for demonstrations. We found out that in those days people expected you to look like a Gung-Fu man.

Gung-Fu outfits in those days were hard to get and Bruce hated them, especially the black ones with all the fancy white trim. He said dress any way you want. Most of us wore what we felt was comfortable for workouts. He wanted no emblems or uniforms when we worked out. Watching one of our classes reminded me of watching a pick-up football game at the park. This picture is typical of ways we might have dressed.

We then switched to navy blue sweat pants with a white T-shirt trimmed in navy blue with the symbol of an empty circle to indicate nothingness.

Our previous T-shirt looked too much like a basketball or baseball shirt, so I switched it to read Jeet Kune Do, Chinese Boxing.

Other design changes in our uniforms over the years. The designs, like JKD and life are constantly changing.

This is the present design used at the academy as of June 1976. It combines the Filipino emblem with the Chinese emblem. The official name of the school is Filipino Kali Academy/Chinese Kickboxing Academy.

This emblem is sometimes used by the Guros (instructors) in the Filipino Arts. Note the small Yin/Yang symbol is the sun next to the triangle. It appears small, but like the sun, has great energy

During the period from 1966 to
1969 Bruce and I often trained with
naval head gear and with finger
boxing gloves, which we modified.

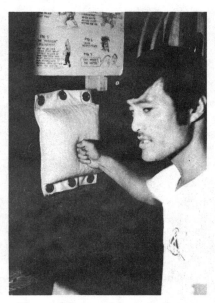

The sand bag used to train the one-
inch and three-inch punch.

This is the original focus glove that
Bruce gave me. It became the prototype
for all the gloves you see on the market
today.

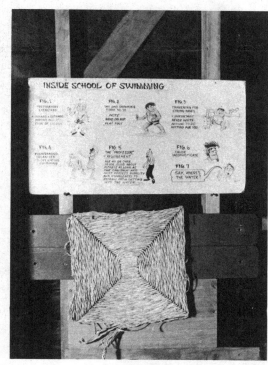

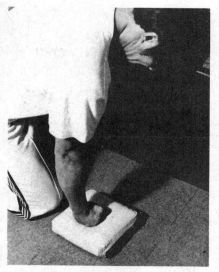

Training with the bean bag on the floor or on the wall.

Straw pad often used by Bruce for hand conditioning.

Shadow boxing with light dumb-bells. Bruce often stressed that I shadow box with light dumbbells.

Another thing he stressed was to train my calves by doing leg raises on the leg raise board. This is Bruce's original leg raise board.

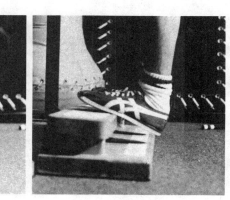

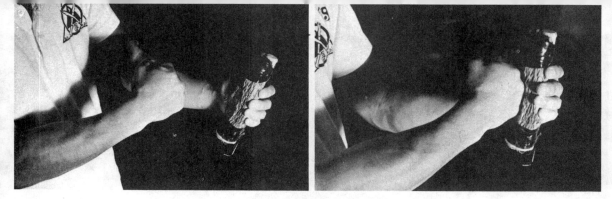

Bruce used this small straw pad to punch while he was relaxing, watching TV or driving in the car with me.

This is Bruce's personal modified Mook Jong.

Gymnastics split straps can greatly improve doing the splits, which is good in kicking.

Bruce said, use "no way" as "way" in training as well as in combat. I have incorporated this training method, called "de cuerdas," used by the Filipino Escrimadores to develop fast reflexes, timing, angling and positions with the stick hand.

To improve my kicking, Bruce advised me to work on placement and accuracy using a small wad of paper or a small ball suspended on a string.

Bruce's original chromeplated push-up handles.

Doing push-ups with the push-up handles.

Bruce's neck and head lock apparatus designed and constructed by James Lee.

Instructor Jerry Poteet demonstrating a head lock on the apparatus.

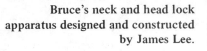

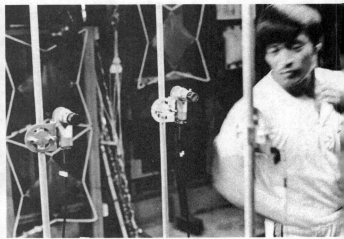

The reflex time indicator which times punches, strikes and kicks in (thousandths of a second)

Isometric training on the power rack. This is the original power rack I inherited from Bruce before he left for Hong Kong.

Portable isometric apparatus which Bruce gave to me in 1967. Isometric training is an integral part of Jeet June Do training.

Bruce Lee's giant heavy bag, made for him by Bob Wall. It dwarfs the boys in the picture.

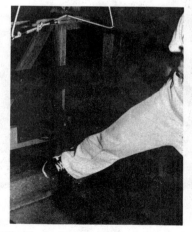

The foot-obstruction and shin-kick apparatus designed and constructed for Bruce by James Lee. Bruce gave it to me when he left for Hong Kong. It's now in my garage.

These are Bruce Lee's finger weights. He used them to develop the muscles in his fingers, and by tying a strip of tape or cloth to them, you can develop the neck and jaw muscles. Good neck muscles are essential for taking a strong punch, and jaw muscles are essential in biting tactics.

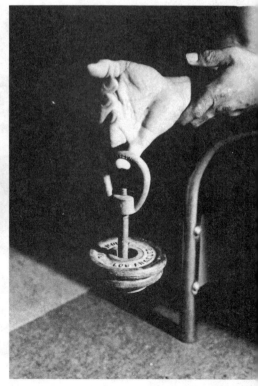

Shadow boxing is one of the best ways I know of to study your mistakes. Shadow boxing limbers up the muscles, it develops speed, endurance and proper fighting form. It also develops your defenses and attacks to meet all the different situations you might encounter. It is also greatly useful in helping your creativity and imagination.

These three pictures illustrate the three-inch punch. From the three-inch punch, the student progresses to the one-inch punch. These short punches are very useful in close-quarter combat situations because you do not have to draw back to gain power.

One of the ways to train for the three-inch punch is to have someone hold two focusing gloves tightly for you to hit.

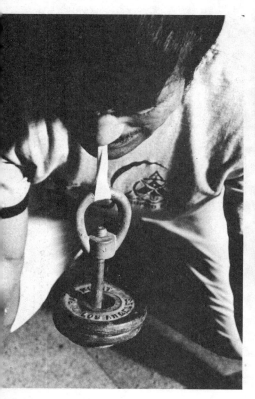

Bruce always felt that the midsection was the window of health. This is just one of the exercises he did to strengthen the abdomen, on the Roman Chair.

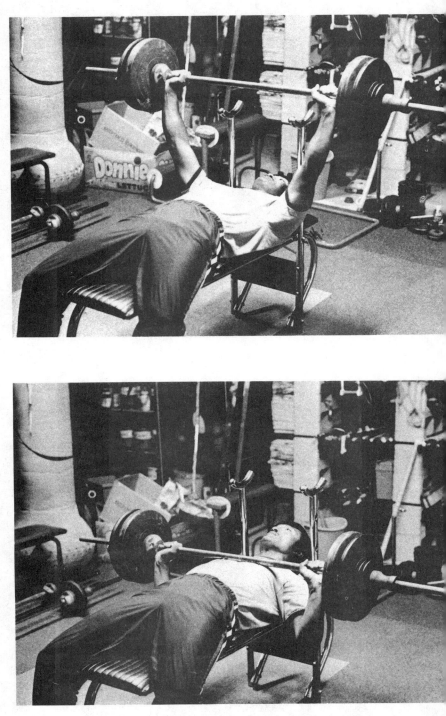

Bruce was strongly in favor of supplementing JKD
with weight training. He used weights to build certain
muscle groups and to perform specific movements
more proficiently. Weight training, then, is the means
to an end and not an end in itself.

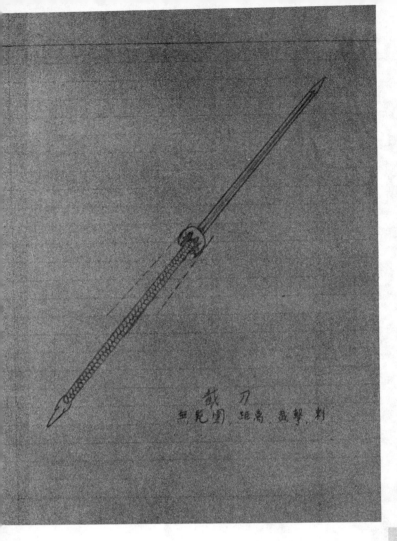

戟刀

無死圍 距離 威擊 刺

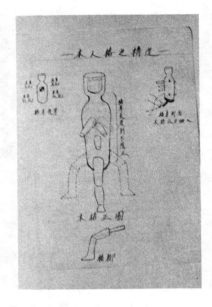

一木人術之精定一

木橋三圍

Bruce Lee was truly a creative and inovative man. Here are some of his sketches. He was always trying to make things a little better. The weapon on the left was called the "Jeet."
It was an improvement over the staff, with elements of a spear and a sword guard.

The shelf of focus gloves at the Filipino Kali Academy. It was Bruce's idea as far back as 1962 to use the focus glove in training. In fact, it was Bruce Lee who popularized its use in martial art.

360° 陳

4″長

Here was a weapon that only he could have used.

92

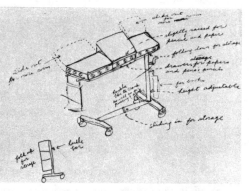

He often sketched
fight sequences for the
Green Hornet in Chinese.

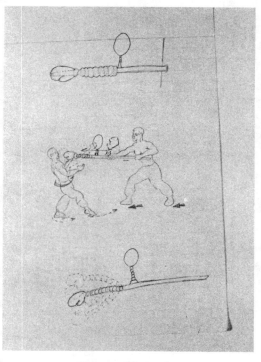

This was his version
of a portable, alive
training apparatus.

Even when he was laid up with
back problems he thought of
a better way to work while
lying in bed.

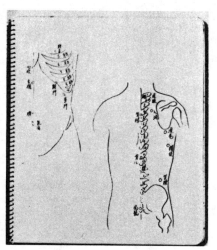

He created, researched
and studied all available
material on many subjects.

illustrations by Bruce Lee

Jeet Kune Do is training and discipline toward the ultimate reality in combat. The ULTIMATE REALITY is the RETURNING TO ONE'S PRIMARY FREEDOM which is SIMPLE, DIRECT and NON-CLASSICAL.

A good JKD man does not oppose force or give way completely. He is pliable as a spring; he is the complement and not the opposition to his opponent's strength. HE HAS NO TECHNIQUE; HE MAKES HIS OPPONENTS' TECHNIQUES HIS TECHNIQUE. He has no design; he makes opportunity his design.

One should respond to circumstance without artificial and "wooden" prearrangement. Your action should be like the immediacy of a shadow adapting to a moving object. Your task is simply to complete the other half of the "oneness" spontaneously.

In JKD, one does not accumulate but eliminates. It is not daily increase, but daily decrease. The height of cultivation always runs to simplicity. It is the half way cultivation that runs to ornamentation.

So it is not how much fixed knowledge one has accumulated; rather it is what one can apply alively that counts. "Being" is definitely more valued than "doing".

The understanding of JKD is through personal feeling from moment to moment in the mirror of relationship and not through a process of isolation. To be is to be related. To isolate is death.

Any technique, however worthy and desirable, becomes a disease, when the mind is obsessed with it.

Learn the principle, abide by the principles and dissolve the principle. In short, to enter a mould without being caged in it, and OBEY THE PRINCIPLE WITHOUT BEING BOUND BY THEM.

My followers in JKD, do listen to this-----all fixed set patterns are incapable of adaptability or pliability. THE TRUTH IS OUTSIDE OF ALL FIXED PATTERNS. Try and obtain a managable shape of a nicely-tied package of water.

When one has reached maturity in this art, one will have the formless form. It is like the dissolving of a thawing ice into water that can shape itself to any structure. WHEN ONE HAS NO FORM, ONE CAN BE ALL FORMS, WHEN ONE HAS NO STYLE, HE CAN FIT IN WITH ANY STYLE.

IN PRIMARY FREEDOM ONE UTILIZES ALL WAYS and IS BOUND BY NONE, and likewise uses any technique or means which serves its end. EFFICIENCY IS ANYTHING THAT SCORES.

When you perceive the truth in JKD, you are at an undifferentiated center of a circle that has no circumference.

—BRUCE LEE 1967

The Way of JKD

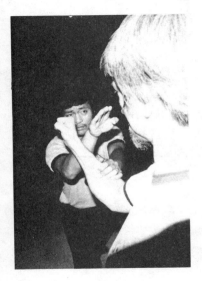

Aficionados will no doubt recall a brief, lighthearted scene from *Way of the Dragon* (shown in the U.S. as *Return of the Dragon*) in which one of Tang Lung's (Bruce) foils attempts to unnerve one of the heavies with an elaborate rigamarole closely resembling a *kata.* Unimpressed, the heavily mustached bully lets the would-be terror have it right on the kisser. . . . So much for the power of intimidation.

Humor aside, this footage does have meaning. For in it Bruce cleverly depicts a major premise of Jeet Kune Do, simplicity, as opposed to extraneous—and therefore useless—motion. And each one of Bruce's films contained similar martial arts "object lessons."

In *Fists of Fury (Chinese Connection),* for example, one of the villains grabs him. Now, most styles would have taken three or so moves to get free. Bruce, on the other hand, just delivers a single punch and answers with simplicity. He also shows that such techniques as the Judo hold are limited.

Also significant is the fact that through his films Bruce was attempting to enlighten the public about what he considered to be a universally beneficial aspect of his Chinese heritage —Kung-Fu. When I visited him in Hong Kong in 1972, while he was busy filming the fight scenes for *Game of Death,* I began to understand why he was pursuing a career in motion pictures with such superhuman zeal. I stayed at his house in Kowloon for about three weeks, and whenever there would be a lull in the shooting we would retire to Bruce's study and listen to music or just rap. During one such occasion he explained that by making people aware of this particular facet of Chinese culture, they would begin to appreciate other aspects of Chinese life as well and that this would ultimately help promote better understanding between East and West.

Action (not violence) was the name of the game in Bruce Lee's films, and the same holds true for his art, Jeet Kune Do. Stripped down for efficiency with the accent on quickness and deception, JKD affords the practitioner a means by which to effectively pursue the most direct line of attack. And once an attack has been launched there are no breaks or interruptions. As one technique nears completion, it starts to blend into the next and so forth—one continuous flowing motion until the conflict is resolved.

Like most creative geniuses, Bruce was only concerned with what is, not what could or should be. JKD *is*. Period. Spontaneous and explosively unpredictable, like a free-form jazz solo, the art was designed to prepare the student for the uncertainties he was sure to encounter in actual combat.

The analogy to the music we call jazz applies on yet another level. Proponents of this new, tradition-shattering sound were initially criticized for their apparent disregard for lyricism and structure; later, when opponents finally caught on, their accolades flowed like cheap whiskey during Prohibition. Likewise, many martial arts purists at first dismissed Bruce as nothing more than a street-fighter and a brawler. Nonplused, he painstakingly outlined the difference between "having no form" and having "no form." The former denotes incompetence; the latter, transcendence, he replied to his detractors. Also, Bruce stressed time and again that JKD was really intended as a means of self-discovery or enlightenment.

In the liner notes to his album Tauhid, contemporary saxophonist Pharoah Sanders describes the process of self-discovery:

"I don't see the horn anymore," he says. "I'm trying to see myself. . . . And all of *that*, all of what I try to do in music, comes back to my conviction that if you have the discipline, you can do whatever you want to. You yourself are the key to the universe."

A firm believer in the liberating power of all forms of artistic expression, Bruce would certainly agree with the above statement.

The most visible distinctions between JKD and all other combat forms are found in its stance, its emphasis on "bro-

Martial arts knowledge, like religion must be experienced in order to be known.

Abandon all the martial arts you have learned.....
In a well not dug, In the water not filling it, a shadow is reflected; And a man with no form, no shadow, is drawing water from the well. A man with no form, no shadow, turns into a rice pounder when he pounds rice.

—BRUCE LEE

ken" rhythm and its eschewal of classical blocking techniques. Bruce reversed the normal left lead boxing stance because he felt you should put your best foot (and hand) forward. He used to watch Muhammad Ali and other boxing films through a mirror to simulate a right-hand lead. Knowing that his right hand was quicker and stronger than his left (naturally, for a right-handed person), he wanted to utilize it to the fullest, so he positioned it where it could do the most damage. This way the right hand could still serve the same function as a probe or feeler that the left serves in boxing, but with the added advantage of being able to take a man out with a single punch (a left jab connects frequently, but rarely with knockout force). And since his left hand was not quite as strong, Bruce kept it cocked back for added power. Or as he explains in the notes he left:

"Because of their advanced positions—they are halfway to the target before starting—your leading right foot and hand constitute at least eighty percent of all kicking and striking. It is important that you be able to strike and kick and kick with speed and power singly or in combination."

In the JKD ready position the right heel is raised slightly to enhance mobility—a must when one is confronted by a more powerful adversary. Particular attention is paid to footwork—bobbing and weaving, feinting—so as to present an undetectable rhythm that confuses the opponent, allowing a JKD man to slip in between his cadence and deliver a telling blow. Traditional blocking tactics are out because they represent the least efficient means of counter. JKD is meant to be organic, alive; each move of itself and offensively inclined. Bruce summed up the on guard position thusly: "Like the cobra, you remain coiled in a relaxed position, and your strike should be felt before it is seen."

As a more dynamic substitute for blocking, Bruce perfected what is now referred to as "trapping hands." Trapping becomes more effective than blocking since there is less wastage of motion and the opponent's hand is fully immobilized instead of deflected. Also, it gives the JKD practitioner the luxury of taking a man out of play, to use football terminology, by creating a favorable one-on-one situation with his attacking hand. Its lineage is traceable to Bruce's original style, Wing Chun, whose practitioners sustain the theory that *attack is the best form of defense.* They reject the conventional one-two sequence of block and counter-attack in favor of simultaneous blocking and punching or *pak sao.*

Chi sao or "sticky hands" practice is a form of sparring not unique to Wing Chun where two opponents face off—forearms barely touching—and try to uproot the other while maintaining their own sense of balance. This exercise, in which Bruce was a master, is performed over and over in order to perfect hand techniques already learned, toughen the forearms and especially to develop sensitivity so that the student reacts to an attacker's advance automatically, without thinking.

Incorporating *chi sao* and *pak sao* with *bong sao* (deflecting) and *lap sao* (warding-off, almost grabbing)—tempered, of course, by his extensive knowledge of body mechanics and motion—Bruce came up with trapping hands. Again, the trapping is definitely Wing Chun, but it's modified. Bruce used to say, "I don't care where it comes from. If it is usable, it belongs to no one; it's yours." That was Bruce. He'd see something he liked, then take it one step further.

To give some idea of just how effective trapping is, I remember a couple of years back when we (the Filipino Kali Academy) entered a girl in the Internationals. She was giving the other girls fits with picture-perfect trapping techniques. She would attack, sidekick, trap her opponent's lead hand, then connect with a punch of her own. Unfortunately, because trapping is a very sophisticated form—indeed, it is nonexistent in most systems—the judges didn't know what she was doing, and so they disqualified her for slapping!

Now, I have to say this about Bruce: In organizing his art, he had all the right credentials. Number one, he had to have been a boxer. He had to have had Wing Chun training to know the centerline. He had to have had a brother who was a fencer. He had to have been a streetfighter to know what was functional and what was not. He had to have had friends in Northern style Kung-Fu to develop his kicking. He had to have come to America in order to meet boxers and wrestlers to reach yet another stage. And finally, he had to have had a personality like Bruce Lee to get ahead.

It was Bruce's habit to forever expound the advantages and disadvantages of the various combat styles—none were overlooked. He counseled his disciples not to think in terms of East vs. West, Chinese vs. Japanese, Okinawan vs. Korean, Karate vs. Judo, etc., for the purpose of determining which was better; but, rather, to examine each method individually, find its pluses and minuses, then inquire of ourselves, "When will this work for me?" In other words, if I have two weapons, a hand grenade and a knife, and someone asks which is superior, I'd reply, "It depends." Suppose the enemy is fifty yards away—I'd heave the grenade. But if we were in a phone booth, I'd be better off with the shorter weapon.

The height of cultivation runs to simplicity. Half-way cultivation runs to ornamentation.

Another, perhaps more startling consequence of Bruce's lifelong research into all forms of combat—from fisticuffs to fencing—was the discovery that, despite the myriad styles, there existed but a finite number of ways in which to initiate an attack—*five* to be exact, all others being variations. He catalogued them as follows: ABC, attack by combination; ABD, attack by drawing; HIA, hand immobilization attack (or foot immobilization attack, FIA); PIA, progressive indirect attack; and SDA, simple direct attack (or simple angular attack, SAA).

The majority of self-defense systems boast one, maybe two, and in rare instances three variations of attack. Two of the most versatile are Western inventions—boxing and fencing (from which Bruce drew quite extensively in terms of rhythm and direction). Bruce included all five methods of attack, bearing his personal stamp, in JKD.

It is a tribute to Bruce's genius that he was so unerringly precise in mapping out the true nature of combat. Granted, anyone who devotes an entire lifetime to meticulously dissecting each and every fighting art known to man could conceivably unravel such subtle nuances as progressive indirect attack. But Bruce went far beyond simply recording. And his ability to communicate his ideas in such a way as to inspire myself and the other students to explore our own creative talents made him the ultimate instructor.

When it came time to apply what Bruce had taught us about the different methods of attack, he didn't want us to feel constrained by any hard-and-fast rules that prescribed which method should be used under what circumstances. The best thing to do in actual combat, according to Bruce, is to let your opponent determine the appropriate technique for you. Again, this relates back to the basic ready position where the combination of the right jab to the head and kick to the shins serves as a yardstick in deciding whether you are in kicking range, punching range, trapping range, grappling range, etc. A JKD man should be able to react instantly and intuitively to any attack by fitting in with—not resisting—his opponent's energy, eventually turning it against him. In sum, as Bruce used to say, *Your technique is my technique.*

He who knows not and knows not he knows not, He is a fool - Shun him.
He who knows not and knows he knows not, He is simple - Teach him.
He who knows and knows not he knows, He is asleep - Awaken him.
He who knows and knows that he knows, He is wise - Follow him.

Senior student Chris Nudds illustrates
a typical solid forward stance used in
many styles of Karate and Gung-Fu.

Bruce once told us balance is when you run like hell to catch it.
There are no fighting stances or horses in J.K.D. Sometimes the heel is up,
sometimes the heel is down, sometimes the toe is up, sometimes the toe is down.
The hands are always in constant motion, the upper body slips right, left,
and up and down.
Stances in Jeet June Do are merely transitions and are never posed or learned
statically. Like a linebacker in football, the balance you seek is dynamic
balance, not static balance.

SAA

Single angular attack and its converse, single direct attack, SDA, represent the ultimate in JKD sophistication. To be effective, they require the utmost speed and finesse. There are actually two types of SAA: one with constant rhythm, another with broken rhythm. Which one to apply is determined, naturally, by one's opponent.

HIA

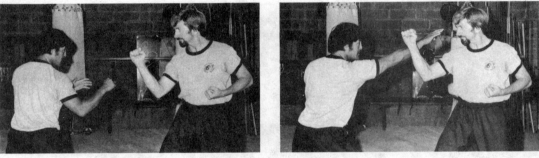

As Inosanto and Poteet demonstrate, "trapping hands" plays an integral role in the hand immobilization attack. By completely immobilizing an opponent's hand, the JKD practitioner effectively

PIA

Distance and timing are key words in the progressive indirect attack. Although the main objective might be a knockout punch to the face, the JKD practitioner knows that he must take an

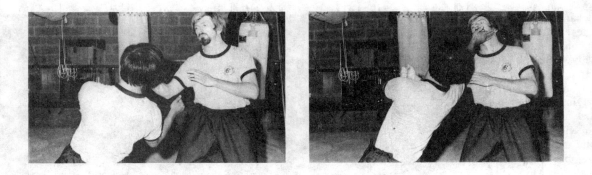

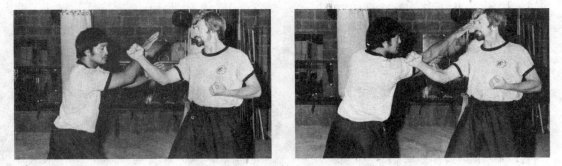

limits the techniques he may counter with. In conjunction with
its counterpart, foot immobilization attack or FIA, HIA is used
primarily as a means of "bridging the gap."

alternate route in order to arrive at his final destination. PIA
usually combines with elements of HIA and FIA as an end
result of "bridging the gap."

ABC

Richard Bustillo and Jerry Poteet practice an attack by combination. There are many variations of ABC employing the hands and feet singly or in combination. Relying primarily on footwork and a logical sequence of attack and counter, the JKD man most resembles a boxer when he applies ABC.

ABD

Before he can even touch his opponent, however, the JKD man knows that he must first overcome a more immediate foe—the distance between them. This procedure of traversing "no-man's-land," of transition and moving in for the kill, is known as *bridging the gap* in JKD terminology. Within a fraction of a second, the practitioner sizes up his opponent—in the process establishing the person's "flight tendency" (a hypothetical aura defining the parameter of any technique he can possibly muster)—and adjusts his rhythm (coordination of hands and feet) accordingly as a prelude to penetrating the other's defenses by catching him at the "unprepared state of mind" (the exact instant one is withdrawing a strike or block

Attack by drawing is counter-fighting. The object is to lure the foe into position for a disabling strike.

or contemplating delivery of same). Throughout this critical period there is no time for wasted movements. One slip and the advantage is lost: your opponent is on you and strength alone will decide the outcome. In order to prevail it is imperative that you always maintain an awareness of the proper distancing and timing.

During the hand-to-hand encounter itself, one is seldom fortunate enough to be presented with a primary target right off the bat. Sometimes you have to attack a minor target in order to get to a major one; that is, you have to inflict pain on a minor target to open up a major target or vital spot. Accordingly, we teach our students that a well-executed kick to the shins can be the passkey to a knockout punch. Which brings up the question of the relative importance of kicking and punching.

Some styles—notably Korean—rely mainly on kicking. On the other hand, practitioners of Shotokan Karate would rather punch it out. In Bruce's opinion, many instructors require their students to spend an inordinate number of hours practicing overly stylized kicking techniques. He took a dim view of the raise-cock-deliver-with-the-toes-pointing-this-way-or-that-way school of thought. He also believed that it was necessary to practice against objects—bags, focusing mits, paper, even trees—in addition to thin air. According to Bruce, there are three prerequisites for effective kicks—strength, flexibility, and economy. The first is developed by running, the second by stretching, and the third by sparring to find the simplest, most direct route to your opponent. Other than that, he said, "If you want to kick—kick!"

In the JKD philosophy it probably works out that the hands are superior. The feet are used primarily as a bothering technique, to close the gap. Again, it will vary with the individual, depending on his speed, strength and flexibility. But on the whole, I think most JKD men are hand men.

Bruce felt that the straight right punch was the backbone of all Jeet Kune Do punching techniques and he wrote quite extensively on the subject:

> "The straight right is the fastest of all punches because the shortest distance between two points is a straight line. With the minimum movements involved in delivery, balance is not disturbed, and because it goes straight toward the target, it has better chance of landing. (The opponent has less reaction time to block.) Also, the straight punch is, without saying, the most accurate of all punches."

He explains that it is foolish, though, to rely solely on one technique:

> "No one punch, not even the efficient straight right lead, can be an end in itself, though there are

styles that use nothing but straight line punching. The straight right is used as a means to an end and definitely should be reinforced and supported by other angle punches (and kicks), making your weapons more flexible without confinement to any one line. After all, a good man should be able to strike from all angles, and with either hand (or leg) to take advantage of the moment."

Finally, Bruce details exactly how the punch should be delivered:

"The way of delivery of the straight right in Jeet Kune Do is different from the traditional classical Gung-Fu. First of all, the punch is never positioned on the hip, nor does it start from there. This way of delivery is unrealistic and exposed too great an area to protect for the user. Of course, this also adds unnecessary distance to travel toward the opponent.

"Instead of coming from the shoulder, the punch is thrown from the center of the body, in the form of a vertical fist, diagonal fist or horizontal fist, and is straight toward the front of your own nose. The nose here is the center guiding line.

"The important point is not to have any classical get-set posture or preparatory movements prior to delivery of the punch—any punch for that matter. The straight right is delivered from your ready stance without any added motions, like drawing back of hand to hip or shoulder, pulling back of shoulder, etc. Practice your right punch from the ready stance and finish again in the ready stance (not back to the hip!). Later on you should be able to strike from wherever the hand happens to be at the moment. Remember, punching in this manner will give you added speed (as there are no wasted motions) and deception (no giveaway movements preceding the punch).

"Relaxation is essential for faster and more powerful punching. Let your right punch shoot out loosely and easily, do not tighten up or clench fist until the moment of impact. All punches should end with a snap *several inches behind the target.* Thus, you punch *through* the opponent instead of at him.

"In Jeet Kune Do you never strike your opponent with your fist only; you strike him with your whole body. In other words, you should not hit with just arm power; the arms are there as a means to transmit from the correct timing of feet, waist, shoulder and wrist motion at great speed.

". . . In advancing to attack, the right foot should not land before the fist makes contact, or the body weight will end up on the floor instead of behind the right punch. Remember to take up power from the ground by pushing off from the left foot. However, the principle or any principle can sometimes be disregarded according to the situation. In other words, know the principle; follow the principle; dissolve the principle."

So to summarize this discussion of the value of kicking versus punching, I would like to echo Bruce's statement that the object is to be balanced. I feel that against an untrained man, it's better to kick because he's not used to it. Against a trained man, against a good martial artist, I say it's better to use hand techniques. Or to put it another way: *Your technique is my technique.*

Thanks to the space age magic of motion pictures, Bruce was able to have his cake and eat it too, as the saying goes. I remember him joking once and saying, "Jesus, where else can you get such a high-paying job doing sidekicks, hook-kicks and spin-kicks?" Be that as it may, Bruce took his filmmaking seriously and worked very hard at it.

Before setting out for Hong Kong in the early Seventies, for instance, where production methods were primitive to say the least, Bruce devoured every piece of moviemaking literature he could get his hands on. He realized that here was a once in a lifetime opportunity and he wasn't going to leave anything to chance. So he boned up on direction, lighting, camera techniques, editing and production to supplement his acting ability. And the ever-increasing demands this put on the commodity most dear to him, TIME, coupled with his feelings that this was not the way to bring out the art, forced him to disband the Chinatown *kwoon* in the latter part of 1969.

For Bruce Lee, acting and martial arts ultimately became one and the same. He was finally able to see his way of life and vocation merge together in harmony. After all, when you get right down to it, a martial artist and an actor are quite similar. For each has to discard his own personality, likes and dislikes, prejudices and so on, in order to effectively concentrate on the task at hand. Whether it be creating a character or defeating an opponent, the mind must first be cleared of all preconceived notions of what should or should not be done to gain the desired effect.

Small wonder, then, that in his movies Bruce is always pictured at the outset as a humble, nonobtrusive individual, and then once the fighting starts he becomes a screaming, ranting lunatic. "Dan," he used to say, "a fighter has to be a madman, crazy."

"I have disbanded all the organized schools of Jeet Kune Do because it is very easy for the students to mistake the agenda as the truth and to take the program as the way."

—BRUCE LEE 1972

This is a sequence of the basic stretching and limbering exercises
we do in the Jeet Kune Do class. Some of these exercises are from
classical Gung Fu, some from Yoga, modern dance, ballet, gymnastics and jazz dancing. We do them to music or to the drum beat,
as it aids in relaxation and helps give us incentive to do the exercise.

The front lock out, side lock out, and rear lock out.

Students training with the leg stretching pulley developed by Herb Jackson.

Rope skipping is essential in Jeet Kune Do. During training sessions students skip rope for three minutes; but on their own training schedules, they may skip rope for as long as five rounds of three minutes each.

Students simulate training with the heavy bag for the photo. In real training sessions, bag gloves are worn.

Speed bag training. On Saturday sessions, students generally go three to five rounds of three minutes each on the speed bag to improve speed, reaction, timing and rhythm. During class sessions, they go at least a mandatory three-minute round.

Instructor Richard Bustillo trains Dr. Bob Ward, conditioning coach for the Dallas Cowboys and former Head Track Coach at Fullerton College, in punching drills with the focus glove. Glove training lasts three minutes.

Instructor Bustillo works with senior student Hector Reid on kicks. The focus glove is used to train the feet as well as the hands.

Student trains for flexibility with a high hook-kick on the football arm shield.

Training session with students practicing thrust kicks on the football shields.

This picture of Bruce Lee hangs at the Filipino Kali Academy. To most people at the academy Bruce Lee is their Si Gung, not their Si Fu. Si Gung means the grandfather of the method and their instructor's instructor. Bruce Lee is also the Si Jo to most of the students here. Si Jo means the founder of the method they practice.

Students practicing the Wing Chun Chi Sao.

The Senior students of Jeet Kune Do going through three-minute rounds on the top and bottom bag.

Senior students of Jeet Kune Do doing basic hand drills.

The hair immobilizing trap.

The elbow and ankle lock used after crashing past the kicking and punching barrier.

Weaponry used in the Filipino arts of Kali, Escrima, Arnis and Silat. We have had many visitors from different parts of the United States, and they are always amazed that the weapons don't just hang on the walls for decoration. The senior class of JKD can use them at any time in practical application. There are no katas in most Filipino weaponry, although they do have a form of free-lance shadow boxing with weapons called "karensa."

Students practicing knife fighting with wooden daggers. They kick, punch, slice, stab and disarm. Training sessions are usually accompanied by rhythm on drums to enhance and bring out the fighting enthusiasm. Instructor Ted Lucay Lucay and I play the drums for the class.

These students are prepared for full contact stick fighting. The fencing face mask is worn over the boxing head gear for more protection.

Applying the "step-over knee hold" supplemented
with the "thumb break" and the "wrist hold"
to a student on the concrete floor.

Full contact sparring session using the "Bangkaw" in the art of Kali.

Every conceivable weapon is used and tested in
actual combat. The action here shows the student
on the left using the "Bangkaw," and the student
on the right using "Sinawali," a Filipino form
of double stick method.

JKD training incorporates the creation of particular situations to develop specific tools. Some of them recreate street-fighting situations, others recreate environmental situations.

Two assailants fight one man, a familiar situation.

This is a situation on a narrow ledge. They are stick-fighting full contact on a bench, using the Filipino arts of Kali, Escrima and Arnis backed with Jeet Kune Do philosophy. They are wearing a Western fencing mask, an American baseball shin guard, a Japanese baton-training glove, a Western cup, Filipino rattan sticks, with boxing headgear underneath the fencing mask. I'd say this is a very good example of joining the Eastern and Western cultures into one.

This is a situation in which two people fight in close quarters with one man higher than the other, such as on a hill. Notice that the man on the trunk must stay as low as the man on the lower level in close quarter fighting. In this art, the empty hand can punch, strike, trap and disarm the stick hand.

This encounter forces one man to defend himself any way he can on his back.

In this situation, two men square off against three attackers. Their object is to get across the room and go through a simulated door together.

This is the fight, the two men against the three. (Note the excessive perspiration on their bodies and hair)

They have fought their way to the other end of the room. The two heavy bags simulate the doorway they must go through together.

Bruce had developed a series of sensitivity drills. These are for visual awareness.

Visual Awareness—the instructor stands in front of the class and draws letters of the alphabet in the air with his finger, and the students must distinguish what they are. This develops visual speed of recognition of movements.

Visual Speed—all the lights are turned off in the room, and the instructor flashes a flashlight on the wall. He moves it quickly, up, down, left, right, and when the light stops, the students either punch or kick at the light as fast as possible.

This develops perceptual speed, or visual speed; it develops mental speed, as they must choose a technique instantly; it develops initiation speed, as they must do it as fast as possible; and it develops performance speed.

Natural nutritional supplements are a definite must in maintaining physical health. Many people will debate this fact and say you should get your vitamins and minerals naturally, but it is obvious that you cannot get all the vitamins you need when training even with a balanced diet.

Everybody has a different body chemistry. Some people need more supplements, others very few. Nevertheless, nutritional supplements are necessary when training vigorously.

This little trampoline, called the "Bio-Energizer," is an amazingly useful piece of equipment for in-place running.

124

We believe music is essential to our training. It is easier to paint to music; it is easier to march to music, and easier to row a boat to the call of a coxswain. The ancient Moros and Visayans of the Philippines trained to drums, Thai boxers use music, and many outstanding Western boxers have trained to music. It sets a pace, aids rhythm and gives the practitioner incentive. Think what a band does for the moral of a football or basketball team.

I have experimented with skipping rope to music, and find that it is easier psychologically to skip to music. Three minutes of skipping rope without music tends to drag, but with music, the time seems shorter. It's easier to drive a long distance in your car with the radio playing. Music sets a mood for action or relaxation. We use slower, soothing music for stretching exercises, and fast, quick tempo when we are sparring.

We use gongs, drums and various percussion instruments as well as cassette tapes. Our music ranges from Chinese, Japanese, Filipino and classical to contemporary pop, western and rock 'n roll, depending on the mood of what we are practicing.

Imagine yourself sparring or exercising to the music of a cha-cha, or Hawaii 5-O, Robert Lee's record, or Soul Train. Or better yet, actually do it!

Bruce called running the "King of all Exercises," because it is an excellent means of conditioning for almost any kind of physical endeavor.

The Art of Jeet Kune Do is Simply to SIMPLIFY

This book was not intended to be a book on techniques. It is intended to lead you to find your own technique.

If you give a student a fish, you feed him for one day and you must feed him again the next. If you teach him instead to fish, you feed him for life.

So it is in teaching techniques. If you teach a student a technique, you must teach him technique after technique. But if you teach a student to find his own technique through the discovery of his own ignorance, you feed him for life.

This sequence is a typical technique taught in many self-defense schools. It is not my purpose to belittle this technique, which will work, but to show a lesson in simplicity and economy.

Compare the time sequence between the two techniques and judge for yourself. In the first technique the opponent gets hit once, and in the second technique, he gets hit twice.

His right hand could have hit directly
with approximately 27" range. But
instead, he wastes that 27" motion
to block inwardly.

He leaves his left hand uselessly on
his hip.

He elbows the opponent, but the opponent's right hand could re-strike
because he has no cover with his
left hand.

Strike directly with the right hand
and protect with the left hand.

Angle to the right and punch with
the left hand.

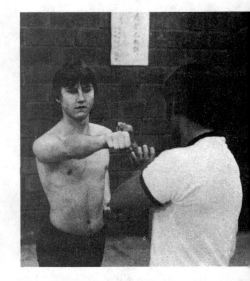

This is a typical block/punch technique used in many different styles of self-defense. #1, the block, and #2, the counter punch. As you can see, he is in danger of being rehit by the punching hand.

A JKD move for the same punch. He slips to the right and parries and strikes simultaneously. The left parrying hand continues to check the opponent's punching hand to prevent its hitting him again.

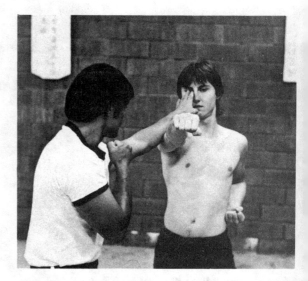

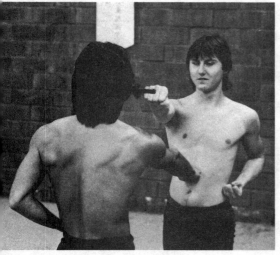

Another typical block/punch technique to the outside of a punch. #1 the block, and #2 the counter punch to the ribs. This punch employs no safety factor.

A Jeet Kune Do counter to the outside. Angle to the outside with a sliding deflection to the eyes. The sliding hand then becomes the cover hand and the right hand punches simultaneously to the body. In the same time sequence, the block/punch technique has hit once, and the JKD technique has hit twice.

A typical block/punch combination used in many styles for an attack of a right punch followed by a left punch.

1. block for the right punch
2. rising block for the left punch
3. reverse punch to the body with no cover for the left punch. In this time sequence the opponent has been hit once.

A JKD counter for the same combination, a right punch followed by a left punch

1. a simultaneous parry and strike for the right punch
2. a simultaneous parry and strike for the left punch
3. a third strike to the opponent with the left hand covering. In this time sequence the opponent has been hit three times.

A typical forearm block on the outside.

A reverse punch to the body without a cover, which puts him in danger of being hit with the right hand.

An elbow strike to the body without a cover, which puts him in danger of being hit with the right arm.

This is a JKD sliding straight deflection strike on the outside of the arm.

The sliding deflection strike becomes the cover hand as the right fist punches the body.

The right elbow strikes, the left cover hand still provides protection.

Compare these two techniques from the standpoint of economy of motion, simplicity and protection. The JKD maneuver includes 3 strikes and 3 covers.

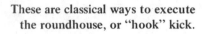

These are classical ways to execute the roundhouse, or "hook" kick.

This is a more economical way of kicking.

 This is a martial artist closing the gap without any fire power.

This is a more economical way of closing the gap, and includes some fire power. He "kick stepped," and now he can jab and trap hit.

A typical technique a person might use which includes wasted motion.

His left hand could strike rather than block. His left leg is closer to the opponent than his right leg, and he is too jammed up for the kick.

This is a more simple and direct solution to the problem. The kick would even be better directed at the low line.

1

2

This is another typical self-defense technique. The fighter on the right uses a downward cross block and a wrist lock.

One weakness of this technique is that you concentrate so much on the technique that you forget about his rear hand punch.

2A

This is one of the many Escrima counters to a block of the knife with two hands. The Escrimador will trap with the left and cut with the right hand.

2B

3

Probably a better solution for
knife thrust counter is this, f
he has angled to the left an
zoned away from the rear han
and countered immediately

It is my belief that it is almo:
impossible to counter an Escrim
knife fighter unless you have
weapon of some sort yoursel

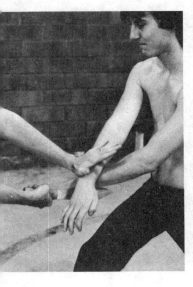

141

"When Bruce died, I didn't know
which way to go. But I feel that
this is the best way - to have some
kind of a line. Funny, but he said,
'When I die, these guys will probably do something that I won't
like. They'll probably build
monuments, have impressive
creeds, hang pictures of me in
the halls and bow to me.' So I
often think about that as I go
through our salutation where the
last thing we do is salute Bruce's
picture. But to me it's an honor,
a sign of respect. To me it's
important that there be a lineage, so
that's what I'm working on now.
I'm going to make sure that, if I
go, there's always somebody. That
is why we're here."

The Path Toward Truth

Knowledge: the accumulation of previously learned material.

Comprehension: the ability to interperate the knowledge in various
given situations.

Application: the ability to use the knowledge in new situations.

Analysis: the ability to break down knowledge so that it can be understood.

Synthesis: the ability to put pieces together to form a new whole.

Evaluation: the ability to judge the value of the knowledge.

I feel that style should be transcended, liberated, if not completely obliverated. Style has nothing to do with the proficiency of a martial artist. It doesn't matter whether he be a Chinese Gung-Fu man, a Japanese Karateman, Korean Karateman, Okinawan Karateman, Indonesian martial artist, Malaysian martial artist, Western boxer or wrestler, Thai boxer, Savate man, Burmese boxer, Filipino Escrimador, Kali man, or just plain old street fighter. The creative mind and the ever changing body is the key factor for any improvement and advancement in the martial arts. Styles or systems or methods play only a part in the evolvement and growth of a martial artist.

In martial arts training. Lead and guide your students to think for themselves. Let them express themselves and let them find the answers themselves. The expression of the self is the art.

An individual can not learn the principal roots of Jeet Kune Do through the accumulation of many different styles; for that would be like a singer trying to improve his voice by accumulating many songs. Rather: it is by understanding the roots of the problem.

—DAN INOSANTO 1969

Beyond Bruce Lee

Those of us who were fortunate enough to have been Bruce's students are grateful for a truly incomparable experience. He was a man of exceptional talent and depth of character, and his remarkable development was an inspiration to us all. James Lee, for instance, insisted that, after studying with Bruce, he felt morally uplifted, more honest, and that his whole life was changed. Another of Bruce's pupils, Dan Lee, has said:

"Bruce was a walking example of the value of basic exercise and fitness. This was the most important thing, because we could see him improving and maturing toward ultimate reality."

Even so, we are by no means the only ones to have felt the impact of Bruce's magnetic presence. He also touched the lives of millions the world over who recognized him as the deadliest exponent of unarmed combat. And I guess that I'm probably more aware of his impact than most because of the telephone calls and letters I receive even today, fully three years after his death. I still get four or five letters per week, and sometimes as many as ten phone calls—all from people wanting to know about Bruce. I used to try and answer all inquiries, but then it got to be too much. Truthfully, I'd have to hire a secretary to really keep on top of it.

Looking back, it's hard to believe that Bruce accomplished so much in such a short time. In a little more than a decade, he had risen from a cocky eighteen-year-old martial artist fresh from Hong Kong to become the first Oriental superstar. By the beginning of the Seventies he was one of the most widely accepted—and worshipped—matinee idols in the world. After the unqualified success of his first two films, *The Big Boss* and *Fists of Fury*, he formed his own production company with ex-boss Raymond Chow. Besieged with offers from all sides—the United States, Europe, the Far East —his salary per picture had soared from a mere $7,500 to

One of my most prized possessions is this pair of foam Filipino "tabak-toyoks" (nunchakus) which Bruce had specially made for me so we could practice full contact without hurting each other. I cherish this pair greatly. Originally there were two sets, but I only have the one left. They are so worn that I keep them only as a memento of Bruce. Bruce Lee was way ahead of his time. He was using real and practice "tabak-toyoks" (chucks) long before they became fashionable.

Many conclusions can be drawn from Bruce Lee's movies. The facts are there but the conclusions we draw as individuals are different. Bruce Lee used a lot of spectacular "theatrical" JKD in his films. **DO NOT MISTAKE** "theatrical" JKD as "functional" JKD.

well into six figures. So genuine and all-pervasive was his box-office appeal, in fact, that *Playboy* magazine saw fit to include him in its year-end cinema review, posthumously, in December 1973. Bruce was called "a major star," "indisputably male," and his Kung-Fu epics were labeled "successors to the spaghetti westerns made famous by [Clint] Eastwood." Nonetheless, Bruce was starting to feel the full effects of success by the time he moved his family to Hong Kong the previous year. Aside from the easily foreseeable invasion of privacy (he often had to don disguises to be able to walk down the street without getting mobbed), something else was gnawing at his insides and it could be that it kept him from enjoying the fruits of his labor as much as he might have. According to Bruce, he didn't know who his friends were in Hong Kong because everyone seemed to want to use him or pester him for favors. He said things were different there, that he had no one he could trust—with the exception of his wife Linda—and that it made him very uptight.

It seemed that everywhere he turned, somebody was looking for a handout, and being the epitome of self-reliance, he found such overtures eminently distasteful. It was a sore spot, and not only with Bruce. His friends back in America, too, were distressed because we recalled vividly the lean times that characterized much of his early life. Yet despite all the headaches, it was apparent that Bruce had "mellowed" considerably in his thirties.

The development of Jeet Kune Do didn't cease once Bruce became a star. While he was living in the Orient, he showed one of the servants, a cook, how to kick, punch, hold the bag, etc., in order to have someone to train with. He still did his roadwork—religiously—and would invariably get a strenuous workout on the set, as the inexperience and ineptitude of the Mandarin camera crews necessitated take after take after take. In addition, having to choreograph the numerous fight scenes stimulated his creative juices, and the inspiration would naturally carry over into things that never found their way onto the silver screen. And then there were the times, when exploring for dramatic effect, that he would reevaluate a certain move or weapon long ago discarded as ineffectual and uncover something that could be used in the real world.

A case in point: As early as 1964 at the first Internationals, I had introduced Bruce to the art of Escrima. At that time, however, he took a pretty dim view of it. Then later when I visited him in Hong Kong, he told me what he liked and what he didn't like about Escrima. I think what changed his mind was the emphasis on the empty hands and seeing through the movies that it had a lot of functional value. And I was really flabbergasted when he grabbed the sticks one day and said, "OK, now I'll show you what I would do." I watched him closely, and with no previous background or training he ad libbed a style of Escrima that he never could have known even existed. Shocked, I yelled out, "Hey, that's Largo Mano." Bruce said, "I don't know what you call it, but this is my method."

Although he would be the last to admit it, Bruce regularly practiced meditation. Being somewhat of a hipster, such "occult" practices just didn't fit his image, so he always played down concepts like internal power, meditation and *chi*. But in the privacy of his own home it was a different story. About three-quarters of the way down his daily list of "Things You Must Do," he had scribbled in the words "Mental and Meditation Training."

Finally, on his frequent trips to the States Bruce never passed up an opportunity to combine business with pleasure. In between meetings, conferences and promotional engagements, he without fail would make time for myself and one or two other disciples. On such occasions he would usually have us feel his gut or some other feature of his well-developed anatomy, making sure that we took note of his most recent advancement. Then he would check our progress, commending us on improvements we had made and suggesting areas that still needed work. And the sessions would conclude with a few invaluable rounds of free-sparring.

It was during one such visit that I saw Bruce alive for the last time. Following a near fatal collapse—due to exhaustion and overwork—while in the midst of the final sound dub for *Enter the Dragon,* Bruce journeyed Stateside for a checkup by a team of American physicians. The incident had received much ballyhoo in the Hong Kong press, and Bruce's spirits were at their lowest ebb in years. But after a comprehensive battery of tests failed to pinpoint any specific ailment, he once again regained his composure. I remember that we were taking care of his dog Riff at the time, and so he came over to my house and we had lunch together. "You almost lost your *sifu*," he said jokingly. "I passed out and my heart stopped." But it didn't seem to bother him at all; in fact, he seemed quite jovial about it. Then he returned to Hong Kong to finalize the script for *Game of Death* and passed away shortly thereafter—exact cause of death still open to conjecture.

Regardless of the ultimate disposition of Bruce's controversial autopsy, one thing is for certain. The founder is dead and the future of Jeet Kune Do is now in the hands of his disciples. When he died, Bruce left behind a tightly knit organization of cooperating individuals and a wealth of written material that, despite his untimely passing, keep the art expanding in new and exciting directions.

The cornerstone of Bruce Lee's written legacy is the recently published *Tao of Jeet Kune Do*. Originally envisioned as a multi-volume work for use solely by his students, it was left unfinished at the time of his death and has since been compiled into a single volume available to the general public. Bruce began working on the project back in 1970, when he was laid up indefinitely after having severely strained his back by overextending himself during weight training.

The framework of the Tao is strikingly similar to the ancient Chinese classic, *The Art of War*. There is no wastage of expression, dialogue is kept to a minimum, everything is concise and to the point. And in it Bruce establishes various truths according to principles which are set out in a challenging, philosophical manner. However, now that the *Tao* has finally come out I hope that people won't mistake the book for the real thing, which it is not. Like Bruce used to say, it is only a guide, a finger pointing to the moon—not to be mistaken for the moon itself.

Another vital source of information concerning the art of Bruce Lee belongs to the privileged few who experienced his

Into a soul absolutely free
from thoughts and emotions,
Even the tiger finds no room
to insert its fierce claws.

No thinking, no reflecting,
Perfect emptiness;
Yet therein someting moves,
following its own course;
The moon in the stream.

Victory is for the one,
Even before the combat,
Who has no thought of himself,
Abiding in the no-mindedness
Of the Great Origin.

teaching first-hand. Bruce was very selective about whom he taught—"If knowledge is power, let's pass it on discriminately," he once told me—and judging from the reluctance of his disciples to capitalize on their training, his discretion seems to have been rewarded. Those of us who have elected to teach certain phases of JKD try to do so with as little fanfare as possible, which means that each prospective student is screened very carefully. Personally, I feel an obligation to spread Bruce's philosophy the best way I know how.

Almost all of Bruce's students had previous martial arts training before being introduced to Jeet Kune Do. Likewise, we require that potential students attain a high level of proficiency in basic self-defense as a prerequisite for just being considered for JKD instruction. JKD training then becomes a sort of a graduate course—an added bonus for deserving students.

All in all, though, written literature and limited instruction—no matter how competent—are not enough to ensure the continued evolution of Jeet Kune Do.

There is, however, a more all-inclusive influence that has tended to provide the impetus for the further development of JKD in a manner befitting the memory of Bruce Lee. Two of the original four persons Bruce authorized to teach his art (himself and James Lee) are gone, and now a new breed is moving into the picture. Some can trace their lineage directly to the founder; others have only read about him or seen him in the movies. Some, like myself, have studied numerous arts for many years, but many have never thrown a side-kick, torqued a punch, been in a streetfight or seen the inside of a *kwoon.*

At Bruce's suggestion, following the close of the College Street *kwoon* to which I alluded earlier, I took four or five students—later on it grew to around a dozen—and we began training in my garage in Carson, California. There we set up three heavy bags, a pair of top-and-bottom bags and a speed bag, and the only difficulty we encountered with that setup came when it was time to spar: the guys narrowly missed hitting the garage door by just inches and it got to be pretty hairy. However, we stayed there until the early part of 1970 when we decided to build a gym in the backyard instead.

So with the aid of a student named Alfred Haber, without whom the project would never have gotten off the ground, we put up a gym that was in every way equal to our present headquarters, only on a smaller scale. Not only was Al a close friend, but he was probably, in the beginning, the most clumsy student and also the most improved student I've ever taught. His connections in the construction field were also invaluable.

But eventually all good things must come to an end, and so it was when my family and I had to move to a house closer to my job. The new home had a much smaller backyard and I said to myself, *Where am I going to put all this equipment?* (By then I had accumulated most of Bruce's old training equipment in addition to that which I already had.) Luckily about this time Richard Bustillo, who had been training with me all along, and I went into partnership to open the Academy because we felt that the Filipino arts had a lot to offer. We also wanted to see Jeet Kune Do continue to flourish, but we didn't want it perpetuated in any way that would demean Bruce's spirit. After much soul-searching, we finally agreed to teach the art. Thus, the Academy was born out of our desire to promote the Filipino arts while providing a rallying point for those who sincerely wished to pursue the path that Bruce had blazed.

Currently our program consists of ten groups—ranging from novice to expert—and a single Jeet Kune Do class that meets behind closed doors on Tuesday and Thursday evenings. This, of course, is a very elite group; new members are only admitted by unanimous consent of the JKD board of directors, which was established as sort of a check on myself so that the power to expand is not vested in any single individual. So far this arrangement has worked out quite satisfactorily, and only those students exhibiting outstanding mental as well as physical attributes ever stand a chance of learning the finer points of Jeet Kune Do.

Bruce never wanted to teach JKD commercially, and he never liked a large class. As a result, I keep the Jeet Kune Do classes small and select the members with great care. JKD classes never run more than eight to ten students per class. And, no tuition is charged. The classes are offered free to the students, but if they like, they can give a donation every month to help support the school, which almost all of them do. However, they are under absolutely no obligation to pay.

Beginning students are told right from the start that what they are learning is not Jeet Kune Do. Instead, they can expect a general self-defense course that includes elements of boxing, Wing Chun, Escrima, Panatukan and even a little bit of Kenpo. The kicking techniques are a combination of Northern Chinese style and Sikaran, the Filipino art of foot-fighting. So it's impossible, really, to put a name or label on what we teach at the Academy.

In any event, a name is just a name—a means of identification. It tells nothing about the efficacy of a certain martial art. Therefore, the curriculum at the Filipino Kali Academy can be described as Wing Chun, Escrima, Jeet Kune Do, etc.— it makes no difference. But I have to admit that the Filipino art, in particular, seems to be a natural vehicle for the maturation of JKD.

In the following, my partner Richard points out some of the basic similarities between the two:

"Both arts stress the lead hand, lead foot. In Jeet Kune Do the front hand takes precedence over the rear hand. Whether it is the left or the right, the front hand is the live hand—the parrying or sliding hand. In Escrima, it's the same thing. In JKD we use the term 'trapping'; in Escrima they say 'checking'."

In addition, there are probably just as many different styles of Escrima as there are Kung-Fu. It is not merely a stick art as many believe. Indeed, Escrima encompasses the entire spectrum of weaponry and is a most devastating empty-handed art to boot. So devastating, in fact, that the .45 had to be invented during the Spanish-American War because a .38-caliber hand gun proved worthless against the Moros of the Southern Philippines, whom the Americans were trying to colonize (in the name of Manifest Destiny) after having been granted the islands as reparation from Spain.

And also like the Chinese art of Kung-Fu, the martial arts of the Philippines are irrevocably intertwined with all facets of the culture at large. In both countries to pursue the arts was regarded as a religious and philosophical endeavor. An exceptional Escrimador had the ability to heel—not unlike the peripatetic monks who traveled throughout China spreading the art of Kung-Fu. Both were treated with awe and respect by the common people, and were believed to possess "magical" powers. They each practiced meditation and cultivated highly sophisticated internal systems. Lastly, some aspects of the Filipino tradition—as with the Chinese—can be traced all the way back to ancient Indian sources. For example, the Filipino word for instructor guro, is remarkably similar to the Indian term guru.

Bruce Lee, in many ways, WAS Jeet Kune Do. His leadership and innovation provided him much of the soul and spirit of the free-form principles of the art, and he will never be replaced. He was the Edison, Einstein, Leonardo da Vinci of the martial arts. Bruce reminded me of Jonathan Livingston Seagull because he was always striving to be better and better. He was a perfectionist, way ahead of his time. Someday, there may come along a person who is physically as talented as Bruce. But I doubt that anyone will ever match the totality of the man, with his knowledge and deep understanding of human nature.

One thing that stood out about Bruce the man was his generosity; he would constantly go out of his way to assist his friends in any way possible. At the same time, he always sought to impress upon us his belief that "there is no help like self-help." Again, I use myself as an example:

I was very shy, bashful, a real introvert, and Bruce helped my personality by teaching me to be confident and more outgoing. He asked me: "Why are you bashful? Have you ever thought of that, Dan?" And I said, "Well, I guess I'm scared of people." He asked, "Why are you scared of people?" And I answered, "Well, I'm scared of making mistakes." He came back with, "What could happen to you if you did make a mistake in public?" and then I listed all the things that could happen—the worst things that could possibly happen. Which seemed to do the trick. I guess you'd call it the Socratic method because he would never answer for me. He would always let me answer.

When Bruce died, I have to admit I wasn't sure of which way to go. I only remembered him saying that Jeet Kune Do had to continually evolve if it was going to improve and keep pace with this rapidly changing world we live in. But I believe the direction we are now taking is the right one, because the Filipino influence provides an excellent foundation for growth and expansion.

I hope it is becoming apparent by now that there is more to Bruce Lee and his art of Jeet Kune Do than most people realize. For one thing, I have already touched on how through the motion picture media Bruce discovered the vehicle he had been searching for all his life to project for the first time ever his art—and through it his cultural heritage—in its true light. And in so doing, he shattered the unfortunate image of the pigtailed Chinaman in such dramatic fashion as to bring dignity and respect to all people of Asian ancestry. For what it's worth, I have been told that in certain countries in the Far East, students have been asked to submit term papers and theses based on Bruce's movies. But that's not all.

With a flair for showmanship that made him one of the hottest properties in show business, Bruce helped millions the world over to put aside their cares and troubles for a while as they lost themselves in the irresistible magic of his artistry. Ironically, we see it is this very same abandonment of "self" —or "destruction of the ego," to use one of Bruce's favorite phrases—that stands as the main goal of Jeet Kune Do training. And it is also the first step in being able to appreciate the beauty of others. In short, what we are striving for in JKD is a better understanding of ourselves and the universe around us.

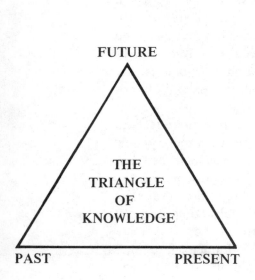

FUTURE

THE
TRIANGLE
OF
KNOWLEDGE

PAST   PRESENT

Like the triangle of knowledge in the
Filipino martial arts, I consider the past
as one of the sources from which knowledge can be found. Much of the knowledge from the past comes from books.

It was Bruce who encouraged me to start
a library. He encouraged me to collect as
many books on all subjects that interested
me. It is from the PAST that we gain
knowledge and from the PRESENT that
we learn how to use this knowledge and
discover new knowledge derived from the
old.

It is from the FUTURE that we learn to
flow with the situation and it is from the
future that we are guided. For the future
holds problem solving situations, and problem solving helps growth and knowledge.

Bruce once told me, "From the old you
derive security, and from the new you
gain the flow."

The books in my library serve as a means
of exploring, researching and investigating
what has been said and done in the past.
They serve as a guide. With any subject
there is constant change, and the wonder
of any knowledge is that it has no particular path. Books give wisdom and philosophy. Philosophy is the love of wisdom,
and wisdom is the proper use of knowledge
and the proper use of knowledge is true
morality. If the world were full of proper
self-governing men, there world be no
need for other men to govern us.

Since Bruce encouraged me to get books
on any subject that interested me, I have
gathered books on my own Filipino culture,
and today, with the help of many people,
I have one of the largest collections of
Filipino books in the United States.

Achievement, recognition, self-respect—these are fundamental needs, without which human beings cannot function properly. And how one goes about seeking to fulfill these needs determines what kind of person he is. Jeet Kune Do is one way; it aims at self-cultivation as a stepping-stone to truth and enlightenment. There are certainly many others since awareness is not the exclusive property of any one method.

In the words of Bruce Lee:

"JKD is just a name used, a boat to get one across, and once across, is to be discarded, and not to be carried on one's back."

This gold medallion is my most prized possession, given to me by Bruce after his death through Linda Lee.

This is a casual picture of Bruce that hangs in my
house. It is a replica of the picture of him used
at the funeral, and was given to me by Linda Lee.

Taky Kimura and Richard Bustillo and I made our first visit to the gravesite of our instructor since the funeral during a recent trip to Seattle, Washington, in 1976.

We were told by the people in Seattle that Bruce Lee's grave is the most frequently visited grave, and that it always has flowers on it. Visitors from all over the world come to see it and pay homage.

At the base of the gravestone lies a marble book.

BRUCE LEE

李振藩

NOV. 27, 1940 — JULY 20, 1973

FOUNDER OF JEET KUNE DO

YOUR INSPIRATION
CONTINUES TO
GUIDE US TOWARD
OUR PERSONAL
LIBERATION

"walk on"

Bruce's favorite words to me were, "Walk on."

On the back of his Jeet Kune Do card, which turned out to be the last thing he wrote to me, he said, "Brother, go bravely on."

Just like water, we must keep moving on, for once water stops, it becomes stagnant. During our lives we have all experienced setbacks, become discouraged, frustrated and have had problems. It is through problem solving and the problem itself that we are allowed to grow. We grow intellectually and spiritually as long as we keep flowing like water.

In other words, "Walk on." This means to walk on without looking back and regretting all the many failures and shortcomings we have experienced, and believe that we are not stuck in the same place that we have been in the past. We all have our problems, but by walking on we can conquer them.

A problem can be used. You can use it to drag you down or you can use it to lift you up. It is better to use your problem and your frustration to lift you up so you can grow mentally, emotionally and spiritually. We all dislike problems in our lives, but they are sometimes necessary, for they bring us experience, and experience brings us knowledge.

Like training in martial arts, there are many setbacks and frustrations. But there is also growth. The true quest of martial art is growth—growth socially, emotionally, physically and spiritually.

"Walk on" is like saying, "Keep on truckin"; or as they say in the Filipino arts, "Keep the chain of movements going"; or as Robert Blake says, "Just keep on strokin'"; or as Bruce Lee says, "Keep blasting." Keep pushing, keep striving, keep flowing in all things, not just martial art.

The Jeet Kune Do family and I have had many setbacks in attempting to bring this book out. At one point we felt it would never come about. But like water, we kept flowing, hoping and knowing that one day this book would be a reality. As a group, we will continue to "walk on," to seek our own personal liberation and to discover ourselves and know ourselves in a newer dimension.

The JKD Family Tree

BRUCE LEE

TAKY KIMURA is the "senior student" of Jeet Kune Do, Inosanto tells us. He was one of Bruce Lee's earliest friends and admirers when the unabashed 18-year-old first returned to America (Lee was born in San Francisco and left for Hong Kong when he was six months old) from Hong Kong. Kimura was originally a Judo man, who was converted over to Jun Fan Institute shortly after meeting Bruce in Seattle, Washington. Currently, he teaches a few "special" students in his private gym.

JAMES Y. LEE had studied Sil Lum Kung-Fu for more than five years before meeting Bruce Lee (no relation) in Oakland, California in the early Sixties. The two quickly became the best of friends. When Bruce decided to open up a school in the Bay area, he put James in charge and, in fact, named the school The James Lee. It was James who prodded Bruce into writing his first book, Chinese Gung-Fu the Philosophical Art of Self-Defense. James died of cancer just six months prior to Bruce's untimely passing.

DAN INOSANTO

DAN LEE is good-naturedly referred to as the "old man" of JKD. Although in his forties, he still mixes it up with students twenty years his junior and usually comes out on top. A former boxer and student of Kenpo Karate, Dan was the first student admitted to the College Street school, run by Inosanto, in Los Angeles' Chinatown. He presently teaches T'ai-chi Ch'uan, in addition to JKD, and helps out with the teaching chores at the Filipino Kali Academy whenever his busy schedule permits.

TED WONG was one of the few non-martial artists to experience Bruce Lee's teaching directly. With no previous training, he began at the Chinatown school in 1967. "One day Bruce saw him working out and said, 'I'll take him for a private student,'" reveals Inosanto. Ted quickly became one of Bruce's closest friends. He now teaches a few private students, worksout at the Filipino Kali Academy every other week or so and has taught Bruce's brother, Robert, and son, Brandon.

RICHARD BUSTILLO is Inosanto's partner in the Filipino Kali Academy. He is a former Kajukenbo man and boxer from Hawaii who first began his JKD training with the original Chinatown group and with Bruce's chosen few on Wednesday nights. Like Inosanto, Richard is primarily concerned with promoting his cultural arts — Escrima, Arnis, Sikaran and Kali — in addition to maintaining the quality of JKD instruction. The personable Bustillo, 32, presently makes his home in Gardena, California.

JERRY POTEET is a former Kenpo man, original College Street student and a member of the prestigeous "Saturday Bunch," who trained at Bruce's home once a week during the Sixties in addition to their regular sessions in Chinatown. Today Jerry serves as an assistant instructor at the Filipino Kali Academy. The silver-goteeded Poteet, 38, is a favorite at the Academy and lives with his wife and children in Temple City, California.

LARRY HARTSELL teaches JKD to a small group of carefully screened students out of a friend's Kung-Fu school located in Charlotte, North Carolina. He first met Bruce Lee prior to the latter's opening his College Street school in 1967, began training then, and continued under Inosanto at number 628. Before that, he had been Inosanto's Kenpo student when Dan was teaching for Ed Parker. Hartsell, a towering individual, is regarded as one of the premier JKD "fighters."

BOB BREMER, age 45, is a former Kenpo Karate student with a working knowledge of JKD. He began his studies under Inosanto at the College Street school and is presently in semi-retirement as far as teaching is concerned. Bremer lives in Alhambra, where he prefers to teach a few close friends in the privacy of his home.

PETE JACOBS of San Gabriel, California is another former Kenpo man who made the switch to JKD once the Chinatown school opened in Los Angeles. Today Jacobs is loath to advertise the fact that he teaches some JKD (in addition to Escrima and Arnis) to a small group of about a dozen in his backyard.

TONY LUNA began his martial arts training in Shotokan and Kenpo Karate before signing up at the Chinatown school in 1968. As is the case with most former Bruce Lee students, Luna prefers not to advertise and teaches only a handful of individuals, privately. He recently passed his bar exam and makes his home in East Los Angeles, California.

STEVE GOLDEN is a Karate Black Belt with supplemental training in JKD. He is currently authorized to teach the JKD method to a handful of students out of his backyard in Eugene, Oregon.

TIM TACKETT is one of the most knowledgeable JKD practitioners, according to Inosanto. He has studied Hsing-I Kung-Fu and various other styles in Taiwan. He also received Escrima and Arnis training from Inosanto, and began in JKD when Dan opened up his backyard to a few individuals following the close of the College Street school in 1969. Tim now has his own school in Redlands, California, where he teaches Escrima and JKD to some of his better students.

ALSO AUTHORIZED TO TEACH JKD:

DR. BOB WARD of Fullerton, California. **SEPH LAMOG** and **RICHARD LEE** both of Reseda, California.

CHRIS NUDDS of England.

TED LUCAYLUCAY studied various Gung-Fu styles and Kenpo before becoming a student of the Filipino Kali Academy in Kali, Escrima, Sikaran and Chinese Boxing. He now has a school in San Diego, California where he teaches Chinese Kick Boxing along with Kali.

The TRUTH IN COMBAT IS DIFFERENT FOR EACH INDIVIDUAL IN THIS STYLE

1. RESEARCH YOUR OWN EXPERIENCE
2. ABSORB WHAT IS USEFUL
3. REJECT WHAT IS USELESS
4. ADD WHAT IS SPECIFICALLY YOUR OWN

JKD Terminology

The Concept of Truth Training: Training that deals with the seeking of truth, this is the highest form of training.

Physical Training: Training and development of the human body.

Psychological Training: Training of the self and the mind for the development of proper mental attitude, to develope courage and confidence and to eliminate all fears.

Unbroken Rhythm Training: Training that teaches various steady rhythms.

Broken Rhythm Training: Deals with the countering of various un-rhythmatic attacks and counter attacks.

Dead Patterns: Training that leads to set patterns and not to the flow of the opponent.

Types of JKD Training:

Agility Training
Balance Training
Coordination Training
Dexterity Training
Economy Training
Flexibility Training
Graceful Training
Finesse Training
Endurance Training
Power Training
Reaction Training
Isolation Training
Environmental Training
Speed Training
Awareness Training
Timing Training
Judgement Training
Kicking Training
Pace Training

Knife Training
Weapon Training
Left-Handed Training
Distance Training
Leverage Training
Linear Training
Circular Training
Locks Training
Lunging Training
Mental Training
Mob Training
Morality Training
Nerve Training
Neutralization Training
Directional Training
Neucleus Training
Objective Training
Observation Training

Kinetics Training: Training relating to the motion of material bodies, forces and energies.

Motion Training: Deals with understanding the various angles of attack.

Pestering : The art of harrassment.

Pillage: The art of stealing time from an opponent.

Piloting: The art of leading your opponent.

Pin: The art of checking and pinning a joint.

Probe: The art of feeling the opponent's movement with exploratory and investigative techniques.

Positional Training: The art of teaching position.

Suffix Training: Training that deals with the ending of the technique.

Prefix Techniques: Fakes that take place before the technique.

Pressure Training

Primary Techniques: Techniques that are most fundamental.

Projective Face: A face that protrudes to draw an attack.

Progressive Combinations: Combinations that progress from one movement to another movement.

Prescribe Techniques: Techniques done in a prescribed manner.

Quarantine Area: An area which should not be touched by the opponent's attack.

Queen's Move: Your best or favorite moves.

Radical Moves: Moves marked by a considerable departure from the usual or traditional, used to throw the opponent's rhythm and composure off.

Rapid Fire Techniques: Quick, rapid firing of the fists.

Rattling Techniques: Techniques used to destroy the confidence of the opponent; either psychologically or physically.

Rebound Techniques: Short techniques used after hitting an opponent in quick, rapid succession.

Recognition Training: Training to develop faster recognition of movements.

Recovery Training: Training to develop fast recovery after an initial attack.

Reflex Training: Training to develop faster reflexes.

Regulatory Techniques: Techniques to control the opponent.

Release Techniques: Techniques for release of holds.

Renew Techniques: Techniques that repeat and repeat.

Reserved Hand: The rear hand.

Retaining Trap: A trap that retains the position of your opponent's limb.

Resurrection Hand: A hand that rises and traps.

Retarded Move: A poor move.

Reversal: A move that reverses the situation, giving you the upper hand.

Rim Shots: Punches and strikes to the arms and legs.

Rolling: Going with the force.

Roots: The main principles.

Runner: A fighter who hits and runs.

Retreating Style: A method of fighting depending on the retreating method.

Intellectually Bound: A martial artist bound by the tradition, and philosophy of a particular style.

Physically Bound: A person bound by the concept of strength and precise technique.

Critical Zone: The zone where combat can take place; same as critical distance.

Sensitivity Training: Training to increase sensitivity.

Set-Up Training: A series of minor blows to set up major blows.

Protective Shell: A shell formed by the art in "in-fighting ".

Tail Gate: To fight from the rear.

Umbrella: Method of covering used by Filipino men.

Undershots: Shots beneath the belt.

Vascillating Techniques: Movements consisting of bobbing, weaving, ducking, slipping and swaying.

Ward-Off Techniques: Keeping the opponent off or away.

Whip Movements: Quick movements characterized by flickiness.

X-Rated Techniques: Techniques used in matter of life and death.

Yoke Training: Techniques dealing with the capturing of the head and the neck.

Set Patterns: Dead patterns, incapable of adaptability and pliability.

Fixed Knowledge: Knowledge that is fixed in time and is not continual.

Totality: The totalness of being.

Partiality: Inability to see or function as a whole.

Un-Crisp, Trash, Garbage: Movements that are not distinct and are often unassuming.

Live Hand: A hand that attacks; a sticky hand; a hand that defends.

Total In-Fighting: Consists of shifty blasting, throwing and immobilization.

Tool Training: Training to develop your natural weapon.

Precision Training: Deals with movements that are precise, accurate and exact in the projection of force.

Central Vision Training: Teaching the eye's attention on one point.

Peripheral Vision Training: Eyes are fixed on one point; attention expanding to a larger field.

Speed Training: Perceptual training teaching the eyes to see quickly.

Mental Speed: The quickness of the mind to select the right move countering the opponent.

Initiation Speed: Speed dealing with economical starting with the correct mental attitude and the right form and posture.

Technique Speed: The speed of the technique.

Alternation Speed: The ability to change directions in mid-stream.

Preparatory Posture: Postures used before the start of the technique.

One and One-Half Beat: An attack performed when the opponent has given one full movement and then breaking the trance by breaking the half beat.

Cadence: Speed regulated to coincide with the opponent's. It is a specific rhythm at which a succession of movements is executed.

Tempo: A fragment of time, like one beat in a cadence which is suitable to accomplish a technique.

Opportune Moment: The time to attack when everything is correct; physically and psychologically when the opponent is weak.

Stop Hit: Intercepting the person's movement during the attack.

Counter Time: Is the second intention attack.

The Fulfillment of a Legacy of Genius

Bruce Lee reminds me of ALEXANDER THE GREAT, who opened the famed Gordian Knot. Gordius was King of Phyrgia. According to the legend, he tied a very complex and large knot with the ends hidden, and announced that the man who could untie it would become the ruler of all Asia. Hundreds of people tried and were not successful. Then came Alexander the Great, who took one good look at the knot, hacked it to pieces with his sword, and declared that he had fulfilled the prophecy. "Cutting the Gordian Knot" is an expression meaning solving a difficult problem in a simple unexpected way. Bruce Lee cut the Gordian Knot of the martial arts world. While many styles said you must do this and you must do that and you must sit in this "horse," "that way," to become proficient, Bruce looked at the roots of the problem, the simplicity of the art, and the principles of combat, and hacked through the knot of ignorance in the martial arts world.

Bruce Lee reminds me of GENGHIS KHAN, the greatest conqueror of all, who conquered the East and West at the same time. Like Genghis Khan, Bruce is loved and respected by both the East and West for his martial arts skill. And like Genghis Khan, his name will live forever in martial arts history.

Bruce Lee reminds me of LEONARDO DA VINCI, one of the greatest artists of the Italian Renaissance. Da Vinci was a genius in nearly all the arts and sciences. Like Da Vinci, Bruce had an amazing knowledge of the human body; and like Da Vinci, he was a good artist. But above all, like Da Vinci, his drawings, designs and his knowledge were far beyond his own time.

Bruce Lee reminds me of THOMAS EDISON, probably the greatest inventor in history. Edison was a genius, and I consider Bruce Lee a genius in martial arts. Bruce invented and devised incredible new concepts in training, experimented with new and different types of equipment, and spent his life in search of more functional, economical and practical techniques for combat.

Bruce Lee reminds me of GANDHI. Gandhi was guided by a search for truth. He believed the truth could be known only through tolerance and understanding of his fellowman. Gandhi overcame fear in himself, and taught others to master theirs. Bruce, in his own way, taught others to overcome fear and to embrace it first so they could master it. He believed that the search for truth in life and in the martial arts was the ultimate goal. He said to me that he wanted his action films to promote the image of the Chinese people, which would in turn promote harmony and understanding between East and West. Bruce had a concern for mankind. He believed that if a man is at peace with himself he can be at peace with others. He felt that martial arts could teach this essential inner peace and that his movies could promote it.

Bruce Lee reminds me of HARRY HOUDINI, the greatest magician of all time. Like Harry Houdini, Bruce could perform sensational and extraordinary feats in the martial arts. Like Harry Houdini, he always accepted challenges and succeeded in being successful. And like Harry Houdini, he knew his subject thoroughly. Houdini spent much of his life trying to protect the public from cheap and fraudulent effects. Bruce also devoted his life to the presentation of the essence of his art in its purest form.

Bruce Lee reminds me of JACKIE ROBINSON, the first Negro in professional baseball. Like Jackie Robinson, Bruce broke through the racial barrier by promoting a Chinese art in the movie industry and making the Chinese art appreciated by the Western world.

Bruce Lee reminds me of JONATHAN LIVINGSTON SEAGULL, who kept striving to be faster, and was never satisfied with himself until he could outdo himself by being faster and faster. Bruce, like this seagull, kept reaching levels upon levels which others said were physically impossible to reach. When people said, how can you get any better, he kept on improving and improving, and improved, physically, spiritually and mentally.

Know Now, publishers of: